JOB MOTIVATION AND JOB DESIGN

Robert Cooper graduated in
psychology at Reading University and
later obtained a PhD in social psychology
at Liverpool University. He is
currently lecturing in the Department
of Behaviour in Organizations at
Lancaster University.

H

Job Motivation
and
Job Design

Robert Cooper

Institute of Personnel Management,
Central House, Upper Woburn Place,
London WC1H oHX

First Published 1974
Reprinted 1977

ISBN 0 85292 094 6

Printed in Great Britain by Lonsdale Universal Printing Ltd, Bath, Avon.

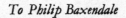

To Philip Baxendale

CONTENTS

CHAPTER ONE

INTRODUCTION

The outstanding feature of organized work in modern society is its instrumentality—the perfection of work as a tool to attain extrinsic ends such as output. From this there follow the economic advantages of high output and low cost which tend to vindicate the instrumentalization of work as well as the psychological disadvantages of low employee commitment and job dissatisfaction which, at the same time, indict it.

The emphasis on instrumentality has many sources. Ellul (1964) traces its origin to the second half of the nineteenth century when there occurred the 'absorption, to a greater and greater extent, of the entire man in the economic network' and the devaluation of all human activities and tendencies other than the economic. Thence arose the validation of the producing-consuming part of man, while all his other facets were gradually erased'.[1]* Another source lay in the rising problems of labour management at the turn of the nineteenth century, occasioned particularly by the rise of trade unionism. Scientific Management was intended by its creator, F W Taylor, to be a rational solution to the industrial uncertainties of that period which would

*All references are given in full at the end of each chapter.

benefit both employers and workers. But '. . . employers looked upon scientific management exactly as Taylor had insisted that they should not: as an arsenal of devices designed to simplify and improve the management of labour. They might adopt the piecework and bonus system, but neglect time-and-motion studies. They might conduct such studies, but neglect Taylor's ideas on foremanship'.[2] This selective approach to Scientific Management, stemming from the desire for a more efficient control of labour, laid the basis for a mechanistic rationalization of work which reached its most sophisticated expression in the theory and practice of industrial engineering.

Yet another source of instrumentality was the need to minimize production costs, especially in the increasingly competitive markets which characterized many mass-production industries. In a United States survey published in 1955, it was found that the criteria used in the design of industrial jobs were based largely on a principle of 'minimum cost'.[3] The three major criteria were: maximum specialization through the limitation of both the number of component tasks in a job and variations in tasks; maximum repetitiveness; and minimum training time.

The distinctiveness of the instrumentality approach lies in its assumptions, firstly that a rationalized emasculation of work is the best or only way of achieving goals of high output and low cost, and secondly that work has no outcomes other than economic ones. This view must be understood as a product of its time. Current views of work are more inclusive. We have, in the first place, a developing body of theoretical knowledge about man at work produced by behavioural science, as well as a more informed approach to the general problem of managing organizations. In addition, wider social changes are significantly modifying the ways in which we define work.[4,5] Economic affluence has led to a diminished concern with satisfying basic needs, while improvements in the extent and quality of education, along with the erosion of traditional patterns of authority, are leading people to think increasingly in terms of satisfying their higher-order needs, particularly those of self-actualization and self-determination. As a result, we are beginning to ask much more from our organizations; instead of us simply serving them, we want to know how they can contribute to the quality of our work experience and personal development. All these movements have resulted in a shift of emphasis from the extrinsic rewards of work to its intrinsic rewards.

Overall, these changes have compelled us to look at jobs from the viewpoint of the employee as well as that of the organization. While earlier approaches to job design implied a technologically-determined view of human behaviour at work, current views state that behaviour is a *joint product of technological and human factors*. From this it follows that optimal performance results only from the reciprocal integration of the technological and human aspects of the job. The interdependent nature of the person—technology relationship is brought out more clearly in the definition of job design as the 'specification of the contents, the methods and the relationships of jobs to satisfy the requirement of the technology and organization as well as the social and personal requirements of the job holder'.[6] This definition also brings out the fact that individual jobs are integral parts of the wider organization, relating individual job holders to other roles in a patterned structure of work flow and social communication. It also implies that, in addition to performance, another important individual outcome of work is satisfaction. This concept of work is further elaborated in Figure 1 which details the human and technical factors of a production system as jointly producing three main outputs: productivity, morale and cohesion. The human inputs are subjected to the moderating effects of the technology to create the three output variables. The aim of effective job design is to integrate the human and technological characteristics so as to ensure that all three system outputs are high. Figure 1 indicates that the choice of an appropriate job design must consider the interpersonal relationships required for effective performance as well as the relationship between the individual job holder and his technology.

Job design, then, covers two distinct but related aspects of work: first, *job content*, the activities which relate the individual employee to the object or raw material undergoing transformation; and, secondly, *job relationships*, the pattern of activities (eg, interdependence and cooperation) which connect individual jobs to each other.

The theory of job design, as we know it today, rests largely on the premise that effective performance and genuine satisfaction in work follow mainly from the intrinsic content of the job. The practice of job design is concerned largely with designing the content of jobs in order to enhance intrinsic rewards such as feelings of

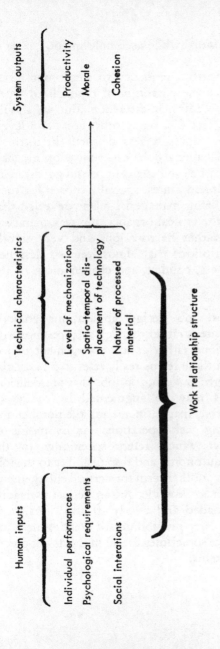

Figure 1

An input – conversion – output model of a sociotechnical system (from Cooper and Foster,[7] reproduced by permission).

Human inputs

Individual performances
Psychological requirements
Social interations

Technical characteristics

Level of mechanization
Spatio-temporal dis-
placement of technology
Nature of processed
material

Work relationship structure

System outputs

Productivity
Morale
Cohesion

achievement and worthwhile accomplishment.

There is of course a tendency to single out mass-production jobs as the paradigm of rationalized work having little or no intrinsic attraction. But we should not overlook the fact that many other areas and levels of work are also more or less deficient in intrinsic rewards. Even managerial jobs can be low on intrinsic content. A survey of 39 industrial firms and government agencies in the United States, specially chosen for their concern with utilizing managerial talent, revealed that 'management in the typical organization was characterized by having rather narrow jobs and very tightly written job descriptions that almost seemed designed to take the newness, conflict, and challenge out of the job'.[8]

Currently, most job design applications embody changes in job content rather than job relationships, and are usually described either as job enlargement or job enrichment. Both these terms really refer to a particular form of job design: building up jobs that are deficient in content. Jobs may be augmented by means of *horizontal enlargement*, that is, increasing the number and variety of existing task operations, or by means of *vertical enlargement* which refers specifically to the addition of skill, autonomy and responsibility to the job. Job enrichment is another term for vertical enlargement. In theory, job design knowledge can be just as readily applied to overloaded and overly stressful jobs or to situations which offer possibilities of creating new job designs such as are sometimes found in the development of new work systems.

Motivation in jobs

Job design theory is only as valid as the motivational knowledge on which it is based. Essentially, motivation is concerned with three features of behaviour: (1) personal needs or wants; (2) rewards or outcomes of behaviour; and (3) the means by which needs or wants are translated into outcomes, ie, how needs become satisfied. The motivational significance of work lies in its provision of the means by which needs and wants can be satisfied by desired outcomes. Job performance requires that the employee manipulates the means offered by the job so as to realize outcomes which both satisfy his own important needs *and* meet certain organizational requirements for effective performance. This definition focuses attention on the key role of means both for effective performance and for need satisfaction. It is clear that performance and satisfaction both depend on the appropriate means being available to the employee in the job. Figure 2 illustrates the process. It begins with the employee's needs, grouped here according to their extrinsic and intrinsic natures. The employee *uses* the job as a means for realizing a variety of outcomes which serve to satisfy his needs. Two aspects of the job affect his ability to realize desired outcomes: first the means available in the job; and secondly the role requirements. *Means* refer to those features of the job which support or make possible behaviours required to attain outcomes successfully. (The absence of means or the presence of constraints will, of course, preclude or limit required behaviours). *Role requirements* represent the organization's and the employee's own expectations of the behaviour required

Figure 2. How the job satisfies employee needs and role requirements

(see text for explanation).

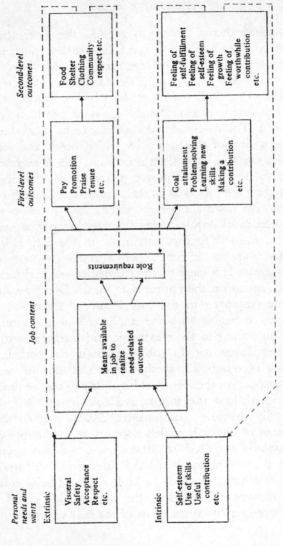

Personal needs and wants

Extrinsic

Visceral
Safety
Acceptance
Respect
etc.

Intrinsic

Self-esteem
Use of skills
Useful contribution
etc.

Job content

Means available in job to realize need-related outcomes

Role requirements

First-level outcomes

Pay
Promotion
Praise
Tenure
etc.

Goal attainment
Problem-solving
Learning new skills
Making a contribution
etc.

Second-level outcomes

Food
Shelter
Clothing
Community respect etc.

Feeling of self-fulfilment
Feeling of self-esteem
Feeling of growth
Feeling of worthwhile contribution
etc.

NB Continuous (feed forward) lines indicate goal-directed processes.
Broken (feed back) lines indicate need-satisfaction and role-maintenance processes.

in the job. Foremost are expectations of good performance and low absenteeism and turnover. The role requirements are, in effect, the standards by which effective job behaviour is judged. The job outcomes or rewards are dependent upon satisfying the role requirements. Figure 2 indicates that means are casual to the attainment of role requirements.

Note that outcomes are of two types: first-level and second-level outcomes. First-level outcomes are those which are *directly* dependent upon job performance—pay, promotion, job accomplishment, etc. In themselves, first-level outcomes have no value but acquire value through their ability to secure second-level outcomes such as food, clothing and shelter. Outcomes feed back (see broken lines in Figure 2) to satisfy personal needs and maintain the probability of occurrence of role-required behaviours.

Extrinsic and intrinsic rewards affect motivation in quite different ways. Extrinsic rewards like money and praise are given to the employee by an external agent, such as an employing organization or an individual manager, in exchange for attaining standards of behaviour laid down by the latter. Intrinsic rewards are under the direct control of the employee himself. A major assumption of current motivation theory is that intrinsic motivation contributes more to job behaviour and satisfaction than does extrinsic motivation. The reason for this lies in the employee perceiving that, under intrinsic conditions, he is the prime cause of both his performance and his rewards whereas, under extrinsic conditions, performance and rewards depend more on external factors. In practice, this means that rewards in intrinsic motivation are more directly tied to performance and are less subject to temporal lags and organizational mediations than is the case with the performance—extrinsic reward relationship.

Sometimes extrinsic rewards are directly dependent on performance, as in piecework incentive systems. Such rewards are likely to inhibit the influence of intrinsically-mediated rewards. In a series of experimental studies, Deci (1972) showed that subjects became significantly less interested in puzzle solving for its own sake after a financial incentive tied to the number of puzzles solved had been introduced.[9] Similar results were observed in a study of the more 'natural' task of writing headlines for a college newspaper which extended over a 16-week period. However, when payment was made on a non-contingency basis (ie, was not directly tied to performance) interest in the task for its own sake remained. In other words, it is not the money *per se* that causes the decrease in intrinsic motivation but the fact that it is administered contingently. Deci explains this difference in terms of the person's perception of why he is doing the task: 'When he is intrinsically motivated, the perceived locus of causality of that behaviour is within himself. He is doing it because it provides him with some sort of internal satisfaction. However, when he performs the activity for external reinforcements such as money, he comes to perceive that he is doing it for the money. The perceived locus of causality changes from within himself to the environment; that is, he cognitively re-evaluates the activity as one which he does because it provides him with external rewards'. The meaning of these findings for job design is clear. Contingency-based methods of administering extrinsic rewards such as piecework payment systems are incompatible with intrinsically-mediated rewards that come from the job itself. Extrinsic rewards associated with intrinsically motivating work should be time-based and not performance-based.

The special relevance of job design lies in its ability to identify the specific characteristics of jobs that will optimize intrinsic motivation. That is, it is able to specify the means that enable the employee to experience challenge and meaning in his work and thus enhance his satisfaction. High performance also follows since it is a necessary condition for realizing intrinsic satisfaction. (see Figure 2).

It should be noted that motivation and performance are not perfectly related. This is because other factors such as ability and temperament also contribute to performance. In other words, job performance is the result of the combined influence of personality, ability and motivation.

Job design for social goals

In addition ot its pragmatic value as a stimulus to performance and satisfaction, job design has an ideological basis. Utopian-minded behavioural scientists and managers see job design as a vehicle for improving the quality of working life.

One aspect of this view emphasizes the value of work for individual mental health and self-development. There is some evidence that jobs of limited content do in fact lead to poor mental health.[10] For example, in a recent study of the determinants of the 'blue-collar blues syndrome' in a representative sample of the US working population, Seashore and Barnowe (1972) were able to show that depression and apathy were due mainly to the absence of challenge in work.[11]

A further aspect of the social use of job design is in the field of industrial democracy. Emery and Thorsrud have pointed out that industrial democracy has two meanings: firstly, formal representation of employees and their interests on boards of management; and secondly the conditions in which the person participates in his tasks and the workplace.[12] This second meaning calls for challenge and meaning in work through the application of job design. Meaningful job content is viewed as a necessary organizational support for the effective operation of the formal representative system.

REFERENCES

1 ELLUL J, *The Technological Society*, Vintage Books, New York, 1964

2 BENDIX R, *Work and Authority in Industry*, Wiley, New York, 1956

3 DAVIS L E , CANTER R R and HOFFMAN J, 'Current job design criteria', *Journal of Industrial Engineering*, Vol 6, 1955, 5–11

4 KATZ D and GEORGOPOULOS B S, 'Organizations in a Changing World', *Journal of Applied Behavioural Science*, Vol 7, 1971, 342–370

5 EMERY F E and TRIST E L, *Towards a Social Ecology*, Plenum Press, 1972

6 DAVIS L E, 'The Design of Jobs', *Industrial Relations*, Vol 6, 1966, 21–45

7 COOPER R and FOSTER M, 'Sociotechnical Systems', *American Psychologist*, Vol 26, 1971, 467–474

8 CAMPBELL J P, DUNNETTE M D, LAWLER E E and WEICK K E, *Managerial Behaviour, Performance, and Effectiveness*, McGraw-Hill, New York, 1970

9 DECI E L, 'The effects of Contingent and Non-contingent Rewards and Controls on Intrinsic Motivation,' *Organizational Behaviour and Human Performance*, Vol 8, 1972, 217–229

10 GARDELL B, *Alienation and Mental Health in the Modern Industrial Environment*, World Health Organization Symposium on Society, Stress and Disease, Stockholm, April, 1970

11 SEASHORE S E and BARNOWE J T, 'Collar Color Doesn't Count', *Psychology Today*, Vol 6, 1972, 53–54

12 EMERY F E and THORSRUD E, *Form and Content in Industrial Democracy*, Tavistock Publications, 1969

CHAPTER TWO

MODELS OF MOTIVES

It is generally held that when needs have been satisfied, they no longer impel men to action. Action is the result of the gap between need and goal and stops when this gap is closed. But this is an overly credulous view of human action. It leaves one with the impression that behaviour is essentially episodic. This is true only for such basic needs as those for food or sex. Motivation based on 'higher' needs such as esteem and self-actualization is continuous and self-sustaining; satisfaction of the higher needs leads to a desire for more of the same. The distinction between the lower and higher needs informs much of the current theoretical work on motivation. It originated in the work of the late Abraham Maslow, an American psychologist.

Maslow's need-hierarchy model of motivation

Maslow's theory of motivation claims that human motives develop sequentially according to a hierarchy of five levels of need:

1 *Physiological needs:* tissue needs such as hunger, thirst or sex
2 *Safety needs:* needs for protection against danger,

threat, deprivation

3 *Social needs:* needs for belonging, for association, for acceptance by one's fellows, for giving and receiving friendship and love

4 *Esteem needs:* (a) *Self-esteem:* needs for self-confidence, for independence, for achievement; (b) *Esteem of others:* needs for status, for recognition, for appreciation, for the deserved respect of one's fellows

5 *Self-actualization needs:* needs for realizing one's potentialities, for continued self-development

The hierarchical nature of the model has two related aspects. First, it assumes that the needs are activated in a sequential manner with a need at a higher level emerging only when the next lower-level need has been satisfied. Thus, safety needs emerge only *after* physiological needs have been satisfied, social needs *after* the safety needs have been satisfied, and so on right up to the self-actualization needs. Second, when a need is satisfied, it decreases in strength and ceases to dominate behaviour; the next higher need in the hierarchy then increases in strength and assumes control of behaviour. When, for example, physiological needs are satisfied, they decrease in strength, and the strength of the safety needs increases.

The decrease in strength of a satisfied need led Maslow to assert that 'a satisfied need is not a motivator'. But this dictum applies only to the lower needs (physiological, safety, social). Satisfaction of the higher needs (esteem, self-actualization) leads to an immediate desire for more 'higher' experiences.

Maslow's theory is both a theory of developmental change and a theory of two different motivational factors. The developmental aspect of the theory states that higher needs develop when lower needs have been satisfied. The two-factor aspect of the theory is reflected in the hypothesis that lower needs decline in strength on satisfaction while higher needs grow in strength on satisfaction.

Despite its wide use by behavioural scientists, few attempts have been made to test the empirical validity of Maslow's model. Since Maslow appeared to be more concerned with the conceptual status of his theory and less concerned with its empirical referents, he did not define his needs with precision or practicality in mind. One obstacle to an empirical testing of his theory, therefore, is the difficulty of defining the various needs in operational terms. This means that not only can there be no guarantee of exact equivalence between the original conception of such needs as esteem and self-actualization and attempts by later researchers to define them operationally, but there is also considerable variation among the definitions used in the empirical research field. A further problem in trying to relate the theory to the work process lies in the fact that people do not necessarily satisfy their higher-order needs through their jobs or occupations; to test this part of the theory in formal organizations would first of all require information about all the life areas in which people seek to satisfy their higher needs. It is also worth pointing out that Maslow viewed *satisfaction* as the major motivational outcome of behaviour and his theory, therefore, is not manifestly relevant to *productivity* outcomes. Finally, a major difficulty arises in trying to infer from Maslow's writings the length of time elapsing between lower need satisfaction and higher need emergence. This could be a long period, perhaps even several years, or it could be immediate, as when a person turns directly from a satisfied lower need to an unsatisfied higher need.

A proper test of Maslow's theory would involve placing individuals who are patently in need of satisfaction on all five need levels in a situation amply supplied with the means for attaining the various satisfactions and then permitting the individuals to choose at will. Such a pure test is impossible both for ethical and practical reasons. In addition, its simplicity would not reflect the important fact that behaviour in the real world is shaped by pressures and rewards which are often beyond the individual's control; his choices are invariably compromises between what he really desires and what is feasible. Unfortunately, Maslow barely touches on the role of environmental factors in the development of his hierarchy, despite wide recognition among psychologists that behaviour can only be fully understood as a result of the interaction of individual and environmental characteristics.

So far, the only direct attempt to check Maslow's theory in an organizational setting is Hall and Nougaim's (1968) longitudinal study of 49 young managers in the American Telephone and Telegraph Company.[2] Four of Maslow's five need categories were used in this study (physiological needs being excluded). These were:

Safety needs: defined in terms of needs for support and approval, security and structure

Affiliation needs: similar to Maslow's social needs and

	defined in terms of the need to establish and maintain 'a positive affective relationship with another person or group in the work situation'
Achievement and esteem needs:	similar to Maslow's esteem needs and defined in terms of needs for achievement and challenge, and for responsibility
Self-actualization:	needs for meaning and sense of purpose, personal development, and stimulation.

Data on each manager's position on each of the need categories were derived annually for a 5-year period by means of interviews. The interview protocols were then content-analysed to provide need-strength ratings ranging from 1 (low strength of need) to 3 (high strength of need) for the nine needs making up the four basic need categories. A second score was also derived to indicate the degree to which each manager was satisfied or dissatisfied in each need category.* Specifically, Hall and Nougaim attempted to test Maslow's hypothesis that increases in lower need satisfaction should be related to increases in the strength of contiguous high-level needs; in other words, they attempted to test the *developmental change* aspect of Maslow's theory. To check this, Hall and Nougaim

---

*Unfortunately, content analysis is a relatively unstructured method of collecting data, permitting wide differences in interpretation between individuals coding the same material. The weakness of the method appears to be reflected in the rather low levels of agreement (as assessed by intercoder reliability coefficients) among the need-strength and satisfaction scores produced by the two coders employed by Hall and Nougaim.

used three methods:

1 *Static analysis*, which involved correlating all the need satisfaction scores with all the need strength scores at the next higher level *within each of the five years*. High correlations were expected between safety need satisfaction and affiliation need strength, between affiliation need satisfaction and achievement-esteem need strength, and between achievement-esteem need satisfaction and self-actualization need strength.

2 *Change analysis* involved correlating changes in need satisfaction from *one year to the next* with changes in need strength at the next higher level during the same period of time. High correlations were again expected between change in satisfaction of a given need level and change in strength of the next higher need level.

3 *Long-term change analysis* involved comparing changes in (a) need satisfaction, and (b) need strength from the *first* to the *fifth* (final) year of the investigation period for all four need levels.

The static and change analyses may be considered as tests of a relatively short time lapse between lower need satisfaction and higher need emergence, with the long-term analysis testing the longer-term emergence of the higher needs.

Neither the static nor change analyses revealed any support for Maslow's developmental hypothesis. Some support for the hypothesis was provided by the long-term change analysis in that safety need strength scores decreased significantly between the first and fifth years, while strength scores for the remainder of the needs increased significantly between the first and fifth years. (However, the increase in affiliation need strength, this being a lower need, does not accord with Maslow's theory). No consistent pattern of change emerged from the need satisfaction scores between the first and fifth years. Overall, the results of Hall and Nougaim's study provide, at best, only modest support for Maslow's developmental theory and, if valid, they suggest that need changes in an organizational setting develop only on a very long-term basis. Interestingly, Hall and Nougaim argue that these results can be better explained according to a 'developing career' model which uniquely describes the progress of a manager or professional in an organization and which is characterized by a series of 'critical' periods intrinsic to organizational careers. These begin with an 'inception' period in which the person attempts to define himself and his role vis-a-vis the organization and thus reduce feelings of insecurity. This is followed by an 'advancement' period in which the major concern is with achievement and promotion and, finally, a terminal 'plateau' period, probably reached at middle age, in which career progress levels off. Although Hall and Nougaim imply that their 'career' model is fundamentally different from Maslow's theory, it would be more correct to say that they have really emphasized the importance of environmental factors in facilitating the development of the needs up the hierarchy.

While Hall and Nougaim's study was not specifically addressed to the two-factor aspect of Maslow's theory, it is possible to use the results of their static and change analyses to check this part of the theory. Since an increase in the satisfaction of a lower need is assumed to lead to a decrease in its strength, one would expect to find negative correlations between satisfaction and strength scores *within the same needs* for both Safety and Affiliation. Also, since an increase in the satisfaction of a higher need is assumed to lead to an increase in its strength, one would further expect positive correlations between satisfaction and strength scores *within the same needs* for both achievement-esteem and self-actualization. Hall and Nougaim's data, however, indicate positive correlations for both lower *and* higher needs, although the correlations for the higher needs do tend to be larger. These results suggest that satisfaction of both lower and higher needs leads to an increase in their strength but the process does seem to be more marked in the case of higher needs.

A need-hierarchy theory somewhat similar to Maslow's but consisting of only three levels has been presented by Alderfer (1969).[3] This theory assumes three core needs: *Existence* material and physiological desires; *Relatedness* affiliation with significant others; and *Growth* using skills and abilities and developing potential. Tests of the theory indicate no support for the developmental-change hypothesis (satisfaction of lower needs was *not* a prerequisite for the emergence of higher needs) but do support the two-factor hypothesis (lower needs decreased in strength as they were satisfied).

In summary, the foregoing studies provide some support for a two-factor theory of motivation, but leave the question of a developmental-change theory open to further enquiry.

Herzberg's two-factor theory of motivation

The differences underlying lower and higher need satisfaction are further elaborated in Herzberg's (1968) two-factor theory of motivation.[4] Herzberg has expressed his theory largely in terms of satisfaction outcomes and he has been less explicit about productivity outcomes. He states that we normally think of satisfaction and dissatisfaction as opposite ends of the same continuum but that they are really two completely different concepts. In Herzberg's view, the factors which create satisfaction (variously called Satisfiers or Motivators) are those which stem from the intrinsic content of the job (eg, challenge, meaning) and which satisfy the higher needs, whereas the factors which create dissatisfaction (variously called Dissatisfiers or Hygiene factors) are those which stem from the extrinsic job context (eg, pay, supervision) and which satisfy the lower needs. Like Maslow, Herzberg asserts that higher-need satisfaction is self-sustaining. However, his treatment of lower need satisfaction differs somewhat from the writers we have already discussed. Dissatisfaction stems from ungratified lower needs but, and here is the important point, *gratified lower needs do not produce satisfaction, they merely remove dissatisfaction.*

The motivator—hygiene theory originated in an interview investigation of 203 accountants and engineers who were asked to describe specific occasions when they felt exceptionally good or exceptionally bad about their jobs. Analysis of the interview responses revealed that the good occasions were characterized by intrinsic features of the job (achievement, recognition, the work itself, responsibility, advancement), while the bad occasions were characterized by extrinsic job features (company policy and administration, supervision, salary, relations with co-workers, working conditions). Specifically, in the good experiences intrinsic sources were mentioned nearly four times as often as extrinsic sources (78 per cent against 22 per cent); in the bad experiences, extrinsic sources were mentioned almost twice as often as intrinsic sources (64 per cent against 36 per cent). Many subsequent studies, using the same 'story-telling' technique, have produced similar results.

Herzberg's theory has been roughly handled by academic critics. They complain that the two-factor nature of the theory is essentially an artefact of the interview method used by Herzberg and his supporters. People are more likely to attribute such experiences as achievement and recognition to themselves and to attribute dissatisfying experiences to external aspects of their environment. It is true that those studies which have used the story-telling method have provided the strongest support for the theory, but studies employing quite different methods of attitude assessment have produced evidence which is at least partly consistent with the two-factor formulation. A possible reason for differences in the findings of the various attempts to check the two-factor theory is that the theory has been formulated in different ways by different investigators. It has been pointed out that there are at least five different ways of expressing the theory, each of which puts a slightly different slant on it.[5]

It is worth noting that Herzberg does not describe the specific means in jobs that lead to satisfaction but rather refers to processes (eg, achievement, recognition) which result from behaviour; in other words, he tends to talk in terms of outcomes rather than means. Specifying the means to satisfaction should help to remove some of the equivocality in the theory. A further methodological shortcoming of Herzberg's approach lies in its emphasis on satisfaction/dissatisfaction criteria to the extent of neglecting behavioural criteria such as performance, absenteeism and labour turnover. A rigorous theory of job motivation must include both behavioural and satisfaction criteria.

Two points emerge from the various studies which have examined Herzberg's two-factor theory. Firstly, there is general agreement on the existence of intrinsic and extrinsic job factors contributing separately to satisfaction. Secondly, there is no consensus that the two sets of factors affect satisfaction in the qualitatively different ways hypothesized by Herzberg.

Expectancy theory and job motivation

So far we have assumed that people will direct their efforts towards the goals which they value. But the existence of a valued goal is not a sufficient condition for action; people will act only when they have a reasonable expectation that their actions will lead to desired goals.

The important role played by expectations in human behaviour has long been recognized in academic psychology. Its application to the understanding of work behaviour is relatively recent. Expectancy theory states that motivation (M) is a function of the expectancy (E) of attaining a certain outcome in performing a

33

certain act *multiplied* by the value (V) of the outcome for the performer.[6] Briefly,

$$M \propto E \times V \quad \text{(Equation 1)}$$

The theory predicts that outcomes which have high expectations of being realized and which are highly valued will direct the person to invest a lot of effort in his task. On the other hand, outcomes with high expectations and neutral or even negative values (ie, disliked) will reduce the amount of effort the person is prepared to invest. And, of course, outcomes with relatively low expectancies and/or neutral valuations will have no influence on the person's level of motivation.

Suppose that a worker desires promotion. Whether or not this leads him to perform at a high level will depend on the nature of his subjective expectations regarding the relationship between his level of effort and the desired outcome (promotion). His desire for promotion will only lead to good performance if he feels there is a good probability that his organization will in fact reward his performance with a promotion. On the other hand, he may feel that good performance will not lead to promotion. This may be because his organization promotes on the basis of seniority or formal qualifications or simply because there are no vacancies at higher levels.

The influence of subjective expectations on job performance is highlighted in a study by Lawler and Porter (1967) of managers in industrial and government organizations.[7] They compared the performance of a group of managers who felt that pay was a probable outcome of performance with another group who felt that there was little relation between performance and pay. Rated performance was significantly higher for the former group.

In reality, of course, a given act of behaviour will lead to several different outcomes at the same time. For example, working hard at a job may lead to a feeling of accomplishment, high wages, recognition by management, and so on. This means that the E X V measure for any individual (E_i, V_i) should be summed accross the total number of possible outcomes to yield an overall estimate of motivation, thus

$$M \propto \sum_{i=1}^{n} E_i \times V_i \qquad \text{(Equation 2)}$$

A study by Hackman and Porter (1968) illustrates Equation 2 in action.[8] Eighty-two female service representatives employed by a US telephone company replied to a questionnaire designed to assess how strongly they believed that each of eighteen job outcomes would follow from working hard on the job (E_i) and how positively or negatively they evaluated each of the outcomes (V_i). Examples of job outcomes used in the study were: being of help to customers; feeling a sense of accomplishment at the end of the day; Recieving compliments and praise from supervisors; receiving promotion more quickly. Respondents answered the questionnaire items on 7-point scales. Individual measures were obtained for the eighteen job

35

outcomes:

E_{help} = Expectancy that working hard would mean more help to customers

E_{acc} = Expectancy that working hard would lead to sense of accomplishment at the end of day

E_{praise} = Expectancy that working hard would bring praise from supervisor

$E_{....n}$ = Above repeated for remainder of outcomes

V_{help} = Value placed on giving help to customers

V_{acc} = Value placed on feeling sense of accomplishment at end of day

V_{praise} = Value placed on receiving praise from supervisor

$V_{.....n}$ = Above repeated for remainder of outcomes

Equation 2 is then expanded thus:

$$M \propto \sum_{i=1}^{n} E_i \times V_i = (E_{help} \times V_{help}) + (E_{acc} \times V_{acc}) + (E_{praise} \times V_{praise}) + (E_{..n} \times V_{..n})$$

The summed E X V measures thus obtained for each individual service representative were then correlated with various individual performance measures (eg, ratings of effort, sales data, error rate). The performance measures were significantly related to the summed E X V measures.

Expectancy Theory places emphasis on the performance—outcome contingency, that is, motivation is only likely when a clearly perceived and utilizable relationship exists between performance and outcome. The theory is therefore well suited to test the assumption that intrinsic outcomes contribute more to job behaviour and satisfaction than extrinsic outcomes because they are under the direct control of the employee himself. In Expectancy Theory terms, we are hypothesizing that the performance—outcome relationship is more conspicuous and more certain for intrinisc motivation than for extrinsic motivation and that this accounts for the greater importance of the former for job behaviour and satisfaction. Several studies support this hypothesis.

Using a complex expectancy framework, Graen (1969) investigated the factors contributing to job satisfaction and performance of 169 women employed on part-time, temporary clerical jobs in a simulated organization.[9] In general, intrinsic job factors were found to contribute substantially more to satisfaction and performance than did extrinsic factors. In a study of 51 US Navy aviation officers, Mitchell and Albright (1972) compared the effects of intrinsic and extrinsic outcomes on satisfaction, effort, performance and expressed intentions to remain in the service.[10] Compared with extrinsic factors, intrinsic factors were much more strongly related to satisfaction and expressed intention to remain in the Navy. Similar, though far smaller, differences characterized effort and performance.

Extrinsic and intrinsic motivation summarized

We have examined two basic models of motivation:

37

the Two-factor model, and the Expectancy model. The Two-factor model distinguishes between 'lower' and 'higher' needs. Higher needs (such as self-actualization) are more potent motivators because, unlike the lower needs, they represent a continuous and self-sustaining tendency for the individual to express and develop himself through the exercise of his 'own forces' (ie, skills and abilities). The Expectancy model says essentially that motivation is optimal when the individual perceives that he controls the means required to realize his desired outcomes.

The main themes of the two models lead us to the following definitions of extrinsic and intrinsic motivation.

Extrinsic motivation occurs when outcomes are mediated by an agent external to the person, and behaviour is perceived as originating in conditions outside the person's control, eg, physical needs. In contrast, in intrinsic motivation outcomes are mediated by the person himself, and behaviour is perceived as originating from his own forces.

Intrinsic motivation: some dissident views

The balmy humanism pervading the theoretical emphasis on higher needs and their importance for job motivation has prompted a considerable body of critical reaction. These criticisms are based on the fact that people differ widely in what they want from work and this means that attempts to universalize the priority of higher needs are scientifically invalid. Some people value work for the possibilities it offers for realizing extrinsic goals such as money or status, while others value work for its self-actualizing possibilities. Job enlargement has been severely criticised for not taking into account such differences and particularly for its implicit assumption that *all* employees want intrinsically satisfying work experiences.

Summarizing and interpreting the inconsistencies and contradictions in the various researches on job enlargement, Hulin and Blood (1968) have put forward an attitude-to-work model, based on alienation or non-alienation from middle-class work norms, in order to explain why certain people respond positively to enlarged jobs while others do not.[11] The work values of the middle class are characterized by a strong concern for occupational achievement, responsible work roles, and a belief in the intrinsic value of hard work. Hulin and Blood argue that white-collar workers in general identify with middle-class work norms but whether blue-collar workers identify with these norms depends on whether they live in urban or rural settings:

'It is postulated that "alienation from middle-class norms" results from lack of socialization to middle-class norms. That is, where a segment of society exists which holds non-middle-class norms and which is large enough to sustain its own norms, the members of that subculture will become socialized to the norms of the subculture. A handful of industrial workers in a small community could not be expected to sustain a separate set of norms, but persons separated from middle-class identification by low educational attainment or low occupational status and living in ghettos, slums and highly industrialized communities could develop and sustain a distinct norm system. Alienation from middle-class norms, then, is fostered by industrialized socially heterogeneous metropolitan conditions.'

Thus, urban blue-collar workers are assumed to be alienated from middle-class work values, while workers in rural areas are assumed to be integrated with middle-class work norms.

At the present time the Hulin-Blood thesis is based largely on inference from ambiguous data which in turn derive from studies not directly addressed to the problem of work alienation. A proper test of their hypothesis would require two important steps: the direct measurement of alienation attitudes held by individuals in the different occupational-community categories; and relating these alienation measures to job satisfaction and job performance. A partial test along these lines has been conducted by Shepard (1969).[12] In his study, Shepard assessed the degree to which 305 workers of different skill levels felt alienated from work. Three aspects of alienation were measured:

1   *Instrumental Work Orientation*, the pursuit of work as a means for achieving ends outside the work situation;
2   *Self-evaluative Involvement in Work*, the degree to which the worker evaluates himself in terms of his work role; and
3   *Commitment to Organizational Goals*, the degree to which the worker values the reputation of his company and is concerned for its efficiency.

The results of this study indicated strongly that alienation from work did not affect the worker's level of intrinsic satisfaction with his job. Alienated workers, just as much as non-alienated workers, were more satisfied when they had intrinsically richer jobs.

The importance of extrinsic factors in work motivation has also been emphasized in a widely discussed study of 229 skilled and semi-skilled workers employed in three Luton manufacturing plants carried out by a Cambridge research team led by John Goldthorpe (1968).[13] After analysing the responses of the workers in their sample to questions on extrinsic (pay, security) and intrinsic (variety, scope for skill) job features, the Cambridge researchers concluded that these workers valued work largely for extrinsic reasons: 'considerations of pay and security appear most powerful in binding men to their present jobs . . . workers in all groups within our sample tend to be particularly *motivated* to increase their power as consumers and their domestic standard of living, rather than their satisfaction as producers and the degree of their self-fulfillment in work'.

Despite the priority accorded to extrinsic factors by the Cambridge team, there is abundant evidence in their data of the Luton workers' strong desires for intrinsically satisfying work. For example: 'there is evidence here that among the workers we studied it was [the] immediate relationship between men and their jobs which was the aspect of their work most capable of producing either some feeling of personal fulfillment, or, on the other hand, some clear sense of deprivation'.

The real message underlying the data from this study is that pay and security are, for this specially selected sample of workers, dominant factors in their *choice of employer*. This of course is not *effort* motivation and, in fact, the Luton study contains no data on the relationship between effort motivation and job behaviour.

A similar distinction has been made by Daniel (1970) in his criticism of Goldthorpe's interpretation of the Luton data.[14] Daniel suggests that there are different sets of priorities that relate to different situations and contexts at work; different contexts highlight different needs and requirements. Daniel identifies two different contexts, the negotiating context and the work context. In the negotiating context, the worker is primarily interested in striking an optimal, or at least equitable, contract for his services; he is therefore primarily concerned with enhancing his extrinsic outcomes. In the work context, he primarily seeks intrinsic satisfactions. Goldthorpe's interpretation of the Luton data is valid for a negotiating context but not for a work context.

It is clear that Goldthorpe not only gives a dominant position to socially-derived orientations to work, but he also seems to suggest that they have a pre-eminence and stability which cannot be significantly altered by job experience. For example, he claims that prior orientations are of 'greater potential importance . . . in determining attitudes to work and the structure of work relationships' than are the effects of technology. Yet there is evidence that flatly contradicts this speculation. Two recent studies of semi-skilled workers have shown that initially negative attitudes to work changed as a result of experience of intrinsically interesting jobs.[14,15]

A better inference from the Luton data would be that these particular workers wished for satisfaction of both extrinsic and intrinsic needs. Such a view is consistent with the results of a recent survey of the attitudes of British Rail employees to their jobs.[16] While 28 per cent of railway workers considered money more important than other job aspects, 66 per cent considered 'other things' *at least as important as money*. Chief among these 'other things' was 'Knowing the job is well done, knowing it is worthwhile'.

Individual differences in response to job content

Clearly, individuals differ widely in their response to job content. These differences have two sources: general experience with the successful use of skill and responsibility; and personality characteristics including intelligence.

Hackman and Lawler (1971) have shown that differences in higher-order need strengths moderate relationships between intrinsic job features and job behaviour.[17] Employees who expressed a desire for greater variety and autonomy responded much more favourably to these job features in terms of satisfaction, intrinsic motivation and absenteeism compared to employees less interested in such features.

Among the more clearly identified personality characteristics related to work content are Intelligence, Achievement and Self-esteem. A number of studies indicate that more intelligent workers are more dissatisfied with, and more inclined to leave, jobs having little variety.[18] Williams has shown that individual differences in risk-taking (synonymous with the concern for Achievement) are differentially related both to satisfaction and preferences for job incentives.[19] Workers scoring high on a risk-taking measure were significantly more satisfied when they worked on jobs which demanded much decision-making and responsibility; they were also more likely to express a desire for jobs which were intrinsically interesting compared with low

43

risk-takers who ranked security of employment over intrinsic interest in work. There is also evidence that the degree to which a person likes and effectively performs a task depends on the extent to which he sees himself as competent and self-realizing.[20] Challenging and difficult tasks are more likely to be assumed and effectively performed by individuals high in self-esteem.

Conclusions

The question of what people want from work cannot properly be answered in terms of simple dichotomies — that one either values extrinsic *or* intrinsic aspects of work but not both together. A more realistic interpretation of the research evidence, and of everyday experience is that people desire a variety of outcomes, both intrinsic and extrinsic, and they will respond most favourably to jobs which optimize the desired outcomes in combination.

People's prior preferences in work must also be distinguished from the specific factors determining their job behaviour. What people want from work may not coincide with what actually motivates them to work. While there is some overlap, the two questions are not necessarily the same. The evidence seems clear that job behaviour and satisfaction depend more on the content of work than on the conditions surrounding it.

REFERENCES

1 MASLOW A H, *Motivation and Personality*, Harper and Row, New York, 1954 (Revised edition 1970)

2 HALL D T and NOUGAIM K E, 'An Examination of Maslow's Need Hierarchy in an Organizational Setting', *Organizational Behaviour and Human Performance*, Vol 3, 1968, 12–35

3 ALDERFER C P, 'An Empirical Test of a New Theory of Human Needs', *Organizational Behaviour and Human Performance*, Vol 4, 1969, 142–175

4 HERZBERG F, *Work and the Nature of Man*, Staples Press, 1968

5 KING N, 'Clarification and Evaluation of the Two-factor Theory of Job Satisfaction', *Psychological Bulletin*, Vol 74, 1970, 18–31

6 VROOM V H, *Work and Motivation*, Wiley, New York, 1964

7 LAWLER E E and PORTER L W, 'Antecedent Attitudes of Effective Managerial Performance', *Organizational Behaviour and Human Performance*, Vol 2, 1967, 122–142

8 HACKMAN J R and PORTER L W, 'Expectancy Theory Predictions of Work Effectiveness', *Organizational Behaviour and Human Performance*, Vol 3, 1968, 417–426

9 GRAEN G, 'Instrumentality Theory of Work Motivation: Some Experimental Results and Suggested Modifications', *Journal of Applied Psychology Monograph* 53, 1969 (Whole No. 2, Part 2)

10 MITCHELL T R and ALBRIGHT D W, 'Expectancy Theory Predictions of the Satisfaction, Effort, Performance and Retention of Naval Aviation Officers', *Organizational Behaviour and Human Performance*, Vol 8, 1972, 1–20

11 HULIN C L and BLOOD M R, 'Job Enlargement, Individual Differences, and Worker Responses,' *Psychological Bulletin*, Vol 69, 1968, 41–55

12 SHEPARD J M, 'Functional Specialization and Work Attitudes', *Industrial Relations*, Vol 8, 1969, 185–194

13 GOLDTHORPE J H, LOCKWOOD D L, BECHOFER F and PLATT J, *The Affluent Worker: Industrial Attitudes and Behaviour*, Cambridge University Press, 1968

14 DANIEL W W, *Beyond the Wage-Work Bargain*, Political and Economic Planning, 1970

15 WEDDERBURN D and CROMPTON R, *Workers' Attitudes and Technology*, Cambridge University Press, 1972

16 HILGENDORF E L and IRVING B L, 'Worker Participation in Management: a Study of the Attitudes of British Rail Employees', Human Resources Centre, Tavistock Institute of Human Relations, 1970

17 HACKMAN J R and LAWLER E E, 'Employee Reactions to Job Characteristics', *Journal of Applied Psychology*, Vol 55, 1971, 259–286

18 VROOM, op cit

19 WILLIAMS L K, 'Some Correlates of Risk Taking', *Personnel Psychology*, Vol 18, 1965, 297–310

20 KORMAN A K, 'Toward an Hypothesis of Work Behaviour', *Journal of Applied Psychology*, Vol 54, 1970, 31–41

CHAPTER THREE

THE JOB CHARACTERISTICS THAT MOTIVATE

In this chapter we examine the characteristics of jobs that draw out and satisfy the higher needs. The problem of identifying the characteristics of tasks which activate intrinsic motivation is by no means a new one. Emery (1959) has discussed several early attempts to specify 'the particular structural forms [of tasks] most conducive to maintaining performance' and interest.[1] These attempts were severely limited in scope. More general approaches either describe tasks in industrial engineering terms (eg cycle time, batch size) or rely upon the raw empiricism of such common or garden concepts as challenge and responsibility. The problem with such terms is that they do not readily lend themselves to scientific study; they are poorly defined and they lack an underlying theory by which they can be causally related to such dependent variables as performance and satisfaction. Elsewhere, I have proposed a framework of intrinsic job characteristics which attempts to deal with these deficiencies.[2] The framework outlines four conceptually distinct intrinsic job dimensions: variety, discretion, contribution, and goal characteristics.

Variety

Variety describes the amount of physical differentiation in the job and its immediate surroundings: differentiation in prescribed work place, in physical location of work, in prescribed work operations, and in the number of people available for interaction in the working area. The variety here is essentially among the prescribed and known features of the job.

There is ample evidence from industrial studies to support the hypothesis that holders of jobs characterized by limited variety will experience dissatisfaction (boredom) and that the resulting need to introduce more variation from sources external to the task will lead to reduced performance and increased absenteeism and labour turnover. There is reason to suppose that the general relationship between variety and the dependent variables of job behaviour will be of an accelerating form with lower levels of variety exerting a particularly degrading effect on behaviour, the severity of this influence falling off gradually with increasing amounts of variety. In other words, higher levels of variety simply serve to make the job tolerable rather than positively attractive.

Much of the early research on boredom in work carried out by the former Industrial Fatigue Research Board was concerned with the effects of limited variety in the job, and increasing the amount of variety in order to reduce boredom. Wyatt, Fraser and Stock (1928) present evidence from a number of quasi-experimental industrial studies to support the view that more varied work leads to greater productivity and that less varied work leads to greater variability of output and less liking for the task.[3] However, in certain tasks studied by Wyatt and his colleagues, such as soap-packing and assembling parts for recording instruments although the more varied conditions generally resulted in greater liking, they led to decreased output. The explanation for this lay apparently in the *less efficient sequencing of operations* in the more varied conditions.

Of more recent studies, Walker and Guest (1952) found that highly repetitive jobs (ie, those low in variety) in automobile assembly were the ones most disliked.[4] Turner and Lawrence (1965), in a comprehensive study of 47 different jobs held by 470 workers in 11 industries, report that their several measures of variety were negatively related to absenteeism.[5] They also report that cycle time, regarded here as an aspect of variety, was similarly related to absences. However, they found no significant relationships between their variety characteristics (including cycle time) and job satisfaction. Length of cycle time has also been shown by Baldamus (1951) to be inversely related to labour turnover.[6]

It seems that variety may assume two different forms within a job and that these may have different motivational implications. In one form, variety may describe the complexity of the *spatial* environment; in its other form, it may refer to the complexity of the *temporal* environment. Spatial variety is the amount of variety within the immediate spatial setting of the job and is exemplified particularly by the variety of operations performed and their cycle times, as well as by features outside the task itself such as the number of people available for social interaction in the immediate work area. Temporal variety in work is usually characterized by a change in the type of work as in job rotation, or by scheduled stoppages such as those designed for rests or meals. In the case of spatial variety, it seems likely that performance and satisfaction will be affected largely by 'stimulus satiation' (a form of boredom produced by continued exposure to the same stimulus pattern). This can be dissipated by perceptual alternation among the various elements in the situation. In the case of temporal variety, which involves change in job or environmental content over time, it seems likely that some form of 'hope' becomes the major determinant of performance and satisfaction. Wyatt, Langdon and Stock (1937) suggest that most work curves are characterized by an upward swing towards the end of the work period.[7] It seems plausible to suggest that hope of an expected, desired change after a period of monotonous activity would be an important cause of such behaviour.

It is doubtful if variety is a true motivator. Its value is probably limited to routine, repetitive jobs which characteristically induce feelings of boredom; an increase in variety simply means a decrease in boredom.

Discretion

Discretion means being free to exercise choice. Discretion in work takes two forms: choice in organizing the means and tools of one's work; and choice of appropriate knowledge in the solution of problems. For convenience, we shall call the former *means discretion* and the latter, *skill discretion*.

In skilled work, the two forms of discretion are functionally related in that the successful application of skill discretion depends upon the freedom to manipulate the backup operations (ie, means discretion) as required. As Blauner (1964) puts it:

'The freedom to determine techniques of work, to choose one's tools, and to vary the sequence of operations, is part of the nature and traditions of craftsmanship. Because each job is somewhat different from previous jobs, problems continually arise which require a craftsman to make decisions. Traditional skill thus involves the frequent use of judgment and initiative, aspects of a job which give the worker a feeling of control over his environment'.[8]

But in semi-skilled work the two forms of discretion tend to be dissociated. Because of the largely routine, non-problematic nature of semi-skilled work, skill discretion exists only at a vestigial level. However, semi-skilled work does offer some scope for the exercise of choice in the way that methods, tools and pace of work are used.

Specifically, means discretion includes deciding the pace one wishes to work at, the methods to be used, and may extend to choice in accepting or rejecting the quality of incoming raw materials and in securing outside services. This form of discretion is often referred to as autonomy or responsibility. Its motivational value derives particularly from the perception that one is responsible for one's own job behaviour and the experience of being free from externally-mediated pressures. These enhance job commitment and satisfaction.[9]

Skill discretion is, of course, a key characteristic of skilled work. When faced with a job problem, the employee refers to his store of appropriate knowledge and from it selects a set of responses which he believes will lead to a solution; this is the essence of skill discretion. The choice of an appropriate response is usually effected through the exercise of logic or trial-and-error. A high level of skill discretion in a job produces a keen sense of challenge which leads, after successful performance, to a feeling of achievement. It is this which makes skill discretion probably the most satisfying aspect of job content.

While there is considerable informed speculation and some anecdotal evidence in favour of the motivational utility of discretion factors in work, surprisingly little statistical research appears to have been done on this topic. Vroom (1962) describes a study relating ego-involvement in work to job satisfaction which, while not directly concerned with the behavioural effects of discretion, does report suggestive data.[10] For 489 oil refinery workers, self-expression (defined in terms similar to discretion) correlated 0.59 with job satisfaction. Lodahl (1964) found that intrinsic job satisfaction among automobile assembly-line workers loaded quite substantially on a 'variety' factor having some similarity to discretion.[11] He also found that 'an individual's expressed intentions about quitting or staying has its highest loading (0.38)' on this factor— that is, men on jobs having more discretion were less likely to say they planned to quit. Of the several task attributes studied by Turner and Lawrence (1965), those which specially characterized discretion—autonomy, responsibility, knowledge and skill—were most significantly and negatively related to absenteeism.[12] It is also noteworthy that the only task attributes significantly and positively related to job satisfaction were again those defining discretion—responsibility, knowledge and skill, and optional interaction off the job. (This finding held true only for town workers; in the case of city workers no significant relationships were found between these tasks attributes and job satisfaction). In a study of the characteristics of scientific jobs in a number of research and development laboratories, Hall and Lawler (1970) found that job challenge (synonymous with skill discretion) correlated highly with the satisfaction of esteem, autonomy and self-fulfillment needs of the research workers.[13] Hackman and Lawler (1971) found that autonomy correlated significantly and negatively with absenteeism in a study of employees engaged on a variety of jobs in a telephone company.[14]

An unresolved question concerns the relationship between discretion and performance. While Hackman and Lawler found small but significant relationships between autonomy and rated performance (quantity, quality, overall effectiveness) for telephone company employees, Hall and Lawler found no relationship between job challenge (ie, means and skill discretion) and performance criteria in a study of research and development scientists. Yet Hall and Lawler did find that job challenge was significantly related (0.48) to perceived pressure to do high quality work. This latter finding agrees with Lawler's (1969) review of ten well-known job enlargement studies (most of which were characterized mainly by the addition of means discretion) which showed increases in job quality but not in job output.[15] When people are given discretion for their work, they are likely to question their performance standards in terms of quality rather than quantity. But neither quality nor quantity can be understood in relation to any aspect of discretion unless some goal-setting mechanism is brought into operation. The discretion in the job affords the freedom for the employee to set (or indeed not to set) a performance goal but one cannot know whether he has or has not set a specific goal just from knowing whether a task has discretion. In other words, performance levels cannot be inferred from the presence of discretion; the level of performance depends upon the individual's response to the job and, in particular, on whether or not he sets specific goals. Only then can we legitimately suggest a relationship with quality and/or quantity of performance. It is worth noting that perceived pressure for quality work was significantly and positively related to performance in the previously mentioned Hall and Lawler study of research and development scientists. It is probable that the pressures for quality work were translated into specific goals by the individual scientists and thus influenced their performance levels.

Goal characteristics

It is assumed that people pursue goals because they value the *content* of the goal. That is, people act in order to gain food, money, promotion, love, favours, or whatever; in so doing they consummate some (usually explicitly recognized) need or desire. Goal-content motivation is often referred to as extrinsic motivation; that is, one performs the task for some reason external to the task itself. But the content of a goal may also cover intrinsic motivation if one likes working on the task for its own sake. Vroom's instrumentality theory represents a sophisticated formalization of the goal-content approach to motivation.[16] In addition to their content, goals possess a certain structure or form which is constituted by *the clarity of the goal*, and *the level of the difficulty of the goal*. It is these structural features which directly affect task behaviour.

Goal Clarity

Performance goals may differ according to the degree of clarity or specificity with which the performance criteria are described. If I instruct a student to 'write a paper for me', I present him with a goal of low clarity; he is unclear as to how long the paper should be and when he should complete it by. The clarity of his goal is increased to the extent that I provide this additional information. In a laboratory study of children engaged on simple addition tasks, Mace (1935) showed that a high-clarity goal ('surpassing a determinate number of computations') resulted in higher performance when compared with a low-clarity goal ('do your best to improve').[17] Bryan and Locke (1967), also using simple addition tasks, compared groups of low-motivation subjects given specific (high-clarity) goals with a high-motivation group whose members were simply told to 'do their best' (low-clarity goal) on each trial.[18] The effect of the high-clarity goals was to raise the performance levels of the erstwhile low-motivation group to the same level as the high-motivation group. Similar results from other experiments are summarized in Locke (1968).[19] In a study of the effectiveness of a managerial appraisal system, French, Kay and Meyer (1966) found that appraisal criticisms which were translated into specific goals were more than twice as likely to lead to successful goal achievement compared with criticisms which were not so translated.[20] And in an evaluative study of a management-by-objectives programme carried out by Carroll and Tosi (1970), it was found, firstly that managers were more favourably disposed toward the programme when goals were clear, and, secondly, that goal clarity was related to certain motivational variables such as 'Increase in effort' and 'Goal success' through a number of moderating variables.[21]

Goal difficulty

Goals which are either too easy or too difficult are less motivating than those of medium difficulty. The latter provide a manageable degree of challenge to the employee and thus draw on his motivation. Locke has summarized the results of a number of studies which he and his colleagues have carried out on the relationship between performance and goal difficulty.[22] He reports that the rank-order correlation between goal difficulty and mean performance for 12 separate studies was 0.78 ($p < 0.01$). This correlation summarizes the relationship between goal difficulty and performance across a variety of tasks: brainstorming, complex computation, addition, perceptual speed, toy construction, reaction time and college grade achievement. Locke also summarizes many other studies, experimental and field, which support the motivational efficacy of difficult over easy goals.

It seems reasonable to assume that the attainment of a difficult goal would be intrinsically satisfying. Locke, Cartledge and Knerr have provided evidence for this assumption from laboratory tasks though no direct industrial tests have yet been attempted.[23,24] It might also be assumed that absenteeism and labour turnover would be negatively related to the attainment of difficult goals if only on the basis that satisfaction would induce approach rather than avoidance behaviours. Again, no hard evidence exists to support the assumption.

Contribution

Most work results in constructive changes which contribute to some end product or service. Contributions derive their motivational value from the fact that they effect changes within the total structure of the task; the greater the contribution to the total task, the greater its power to motivate. In addition, the effects of contributions must be unequivocally perceived by the performer in order to maximise their motivational value. Contributions, then, can be viewed firstly in terms of their effectance value or the extent to which they contribute to the total task, and, second, their feedback or distinctness of their perceived effects.

A common assertion embodying the idea of contribution is that 'whole' tasks, in contrast to 'part' tasks, are more motivating and more satisfying to perform. (A definition of 'whole' task is presented below in the section on group tasks.) However, it is not the fact of 'wholeness' that is important but the significance of the contribution within the overall structure of the product or service. Consider the task of completing a jigsaw puzzle. Our imaginary performer begins by selecting all those pieces having at least one straight side; his strategy is to complete first the outside frame of the puzzle and then fill in the middle 'picture' pieces. In these early stages the fitting together of each jigsaw piece does not add spectacularly to the total puzzle, but, as the salient characteristics of the picture emerge, each added piece contributes more significantly to the task, its significance being proportional to the extent of the information it adds. Many organizational jobs are like this. Compare the job of press operator in a car factory whose machine presses out car doors from sheet steel with the job of the assembler who fixes the same doors to the visible car body. The latter job contributes *centrally* to the total configuration of the product whereas the former contributes only *peripherally*. Adding a door or a steering column or a wheel represent important contributions to the manufacture of the vehicle. Early production contributions have little value because they do not contribute visibly to the vehicle's *essential* character. Equally, contributions which come late in the production process add relatively little because at this stage the vehicle's essential character has been established for some time.

Surprisingly few studies have examined the implications of the contribution concept for job behaviour. Turner and Lawrence (1965) used the concept of task identity, a composite of both contribution value and feedback, as a means of distinguishing a task 'as a unique and visible work assignment'.[25] They found that, while task identity was negatively associated with absenteeism, it was unrelated to job satisfaction. Hackman and Lawler (1971) used task identity (which they defined largely in terms of the extent to which the employee can do a 'whole' piece of work) and feedback as separate task characteristic measures.[26] In their study, task identity was significantly related to: rated overall performance effectiveness (0.11, $p < 0.05$), absenteeism (—0.22, $p < 0.05$), and various specific satisfaction items such as 'feeling of worthwhile accomplishment' (0.28, $p < 0.05$) and 'self-esteem obtained from job' (0.15, $p < 0.05$). In contrast, feedback was neither related to performance nor absenteeism but was clearly related to items such as 'Feeling of worthwhile accomplishment' (0.42, $p < 0.05$) and 'self-esteem obtained from job' (0.35, $p < 0.05$).

The job characteristics combined

Writing on the Bell Telephone System's experience with job design, Robert Ford (1969) has suggested that job characteristics have to combine in order to motivate employees: 'Perhaps they have the effect of a shotgun blast; it is the whole charge that brings the beast down'.[27] But exactly how do they combine? Do they have a multiplicative effect on job behaviour or are their effects additive? In the multiplicative model, the interaction effects between the various characteristics are large compared to the effects of single characteristics. In the additive model, the effects of single characteristics are larger than the effects of the various characteristics in interaction.

Patchen's (1970) study of a wide variety of jobs in the Tennessee Valley Authority has produced clear support for the additive model.[28] While his data indicate that some interaction effects occurred for certain job characteristics, these were small in value and few in number. Job characteristics such as control over means and job difficulty, operating independently, had an overwhelmingly greater influence on job behaviour. This suggests that increases in one job characteristic can induce increases in employee motivation even when other characteristics remain unchanged.

However, each of the individual characteristics of our framework implies a unique consequence for job behaviour, as we noted above. Variety benefits performance and satisfaction by reducing the inhibiting effects of boredom. At best, it makes the job tolerable rather than positively motivating. Skill discretion is the characteristic most likely to produce achievement feelings, while the influence of means discretion is especially marked in job commitment. Goal clarity and difficulty are the characteristics most directly related to performance. Contribution adds meaning to one's job activities and thereby enhances feelings of worthwhile accomplishment.

Maximum motivation seems likely only when all four characteristics are amply represented in the job (with variety being the least important). This follows first from the largely additive effects of the individual characteristics, and, secondly, the apparent fact that they influence job behaviour in different ways. Supporting this generalization are data from Hackman and Lawler's comparisons of telephone company employee reactions to (a) jobs uniformly high on all such characteristics, (b) jobs uniformly low on all such characteristics and (c) jobs high on some characteristics and low on others.[29] Performance and satisfaction were highest under (a), lowest under (b), and intermediate under (c).

The organization and motivation of group tasks

Tasks are often organized on a group basis. This occurs when the task is too complex for an individual to perform in the required time. The complex task is broken down into smaller part-tasks which are shared among a number of individuals. A group task is defined in terms of interdependence between part-tasks, and the existence of a common goal, as with a team of doctors and nurses conducting a surgical operation.

The form of interdependence and coordination in the group depends on the degree of complexity of the group task. Complexity itself is defined first in terms of predictability/unpredictability, ie, variability over time, and secondly degree of similarity/dissimilarity between constituent elements of the task. In highly complex tasks (ie, those that are unpredictable and consist of many dissimilar elements), interdependence tends to be reciprocal. That is, group members contribute reciprocally to each other's activities, and coordination tends to be by *mutual adjustment*, with group members adjusting their activities to each other on the basis of variable task demands. In less complex group tasks, interdependence tends to be sequential, that is activities take a serial form, and coordination is usually by *plan* with rules which govern members' interdependent actions.

Another requirement of highly complex group tasks is that individual group members should be capable of carrying out a variety of task functions. This is important, not just because the intrinsic variability of complex tasks requires a commensurate degree of task variety within the group, but also because it reduces the difficulty of coordinating the highly interdependent individual roles.

The point I wish to emphasize here is that the above organizational requirements must be satisfied before we can start thinking of group tasks in motivational terms. In other words, the creation of motivated work groups requires two basic steps: the integration of member activities with task requirements to give a good 'organizational fit'; and a superstructure of intrinsically motivating characteristics such as we have presented above.

Group tasks generally have more potential to motivate than individual-based tasks. For example, Emery writes:

'There is much greater scope in the development of group responsibility for group tasks. If the individual's tasks are genuinely interdependent with the group task then it is possible for the individual to be meaningfully related to his personal activity through this group task. A group task with its greater size and complexity is more likely to provide structural conditions conducive to goal setting and striving. If it has a measure of autonomy and a wide sharing of the skills needed for its task, a group is also able to provide a degree of continuity in performance that is unlikely to be achieved by individuals or an aggregation of individuals under the control of a supervisor.'[30]

Of the four job characteristics described above, variety has the least relevance to group motivation. Group task conditions may have a marginally greater advantage over individual task conditions in the provision of variety. Where individual jobs in the group are different, job rotation becomes a possible source of variety. Wyatt, Fraser and Stock, for example, showed that systematic rotation of tasks in two-person groups engaged on tobacco weighing added appreciably to performance and satisfaction.[31] Group conditions may also more conveniently provide the stimulation of social contact where individual job content is limited.

In contrast, discretion is well suited to group tasks. Most work on group discretion has been expressed in terms of group autonomy or responsibility. In our terminology, this is means discretion. Gulowsen (1972) has identified seven areas where group discretion may apply.[32] These are when:

1 The group can influence the formulation of its goals, including qualitative, and quantitative aspects of goals

2 Provided that the wider organizational requirements are met, the group can decide where to work, when to work, and which other activities it wishes to engage in

3 The group chooses the production method

4 The group decides its own internal allocation of tasks between members

5 The group chooses its own membership

6 The group chooses its own leader

7 The group members decide how the work opera-

tions should be carried out. (Strictly speaking, this is a feature of individual jobs; group discretion over work methods is covered by item (3) above)

It is clear that the above list extends beyond the group's relationship with its primary task, for it includes certain boundary responsibilities such as choice of membership and leadership. In other words, *full* group discretion is best seen as a process of self-management rather than a limited concern with performance requirements. Implied here is a distinction between a group's *core region* and its *service region*. The core region comprises the primary task of the group, while the service region includes all activities needed for work on the primary task to proceed.

Skill discretion in groups occurs when problem-solving activities of individual members are co-ordinated on a mutual adjustment basis, ie, where the skill and knowledge of each group member serves to improve and amplify the problem-solving behaviour of other members in relation to the group problem. A required condition is that group members should possess different kinds of skill and experience, in other words, there should be some minimal level of role differentiation within the group.

In a group task, members' motivations stem from two sources: first the use of group goals to obtain satisfactions of personal needs, and second identification with the group itself and its goals. Group identification is based on *high unity* (members are aware of it as a group) and *high cohesiveness* (members are attracted to the group). Zander (1971) has shown that groups with strong identification are more likely to set goals that are both clear and are of medium levels of difficulty and to accomplish them successfully. Also, feedback on goal attainment has a stronger influence on group motivation when it is related to 'the score of the group as a whole and of each individual member . . . than either of these two types of information separately'.[33]

Group tasks are often more able than individual tasks to provide a sense of contribution to the individual worker. Rice (1958) emphasizes the need to develop work groups around 'whole' tasks.[34] Division of work is a definitive feature of organization and it necessarily entails the partitioning of individual contributions *vis-a-vis* the total task. Motivation problems emerge when subdivision becomes excessive. Some sense of task 'wholeness' can be retained through the creation of organizational sub-systems having discrete sub-tasks within the total task. Sub-systems are essentially sets of role relationships which cluster around sub-tasks.

Sub-tasks possess wholeness to the extent that they have clearly identifiable boundaries which individuate them from the rest of the organizational setting. Technology, territory and time are the most commonly observed task boundaries and have been described by Miller (1959).[34] Rice was able to create 'wholeness' in group tasks in an Indian textile mill by grouping interdependent tasks together and thus produce mutually reinforcing technological and territorial task boundaries.[35] Time acts as a boundary when the length of the working unit (day, week) is the same as the working period of the individual or group. In multi-shift work systems (eg, continuous processes) the length of the working unit exceeds the normal work period of the group so that time is not experienced as a boundary which contributes to a sense of task wholeness.

Task characteristics and task structure

Tasks have an internal structure. In organizational terms, this structure is expressed as a series of sequential functions: *planning* (setting goals, solving problems, organizing resources); *executing* (carrying out the plan); and *controlling* (evaluating progress and correcting variances).

The plan—execute—control module provides an integrating framework for our individual task characteristics; it helps us to understand them as attributes of interrelated functions which are serially organized within the task.

Ideally, an individual or work group should have a complete plan—execute—control module as its task. In practice, it is often the case that the functions are separated and allocated to different individuals and groups so that managers, for example, are responsible for plan—control functions while execute functions are allocated to subordinate roles.

A fully integrated task is one where the individual or group has a complete plan—execute—control module which is further reinforced by congruent technology, territory and time boundaries.

REFERENCES

1 EMERY F E, *Characteristics of Socio-technical Systems*, Tavistock Institute of Human Relations, 1959

2 COOPER R, 'Task Characteristics and Intrinsic Motivation', *Human Relations*, Vol 26, 1973, 387–413

3 WYATT S, FRASER J A and STOCK F G L, *The Comparative Effects of Variety and Uniformity in Work*, HMSO, London, 1928

WYATT S and OGDEN D A, *On the Extent and Effects of Variety and Uniformity in Repetitive Work*, HMSO, 1924

4 WALKER C R and GUEST R H, *The Man on the Assembly Line*, Harvard University Press, Cambridge, Mass, 1952

5 TURNER A N and LAWRENCE P R, *Industrial Jobs and the Worker: an Investigation of Response to Task Attributes*, Harvard University Graduate School of Business Administration, Boston, 1965

6 BALDAMUS W, 'Type of Work and Motivation', *British Journal of Sociology*, Vol 2, 1951, 44–58

7 WYATT S, LANGDON J N and STOCK F G L, *Fatigue and Boredom in Repetitive Work*, HMSO, 1937

8 BLAUNER R, *Alienation and Freedom: The Factory Worker and his Industry*, University of Chicago Press, Chicago, 1964

9 For a theoretical discussion of this point, see KIESLER C, *The Psychology of Commitment*, Academic Press, New York, 1971, especially pp. 167–168

10 VROOM V H, 'Ego-involvement, Job Satisfaction and Job Performance, *Personnel Psychology*, Vol 15, 1962, 159–177

11 LODAHL T M, 'Patterns of Job Attitudes in Two Assembly Technologies', *Administrative Science Quarterly*, Vol 8, 1964, 483–519

12 TURNER and LAWRENCE, *Op cit*

13 HALL D T and LAWLER E E, 'Job Characteristics and Pressures and the Organizational Integration of Professionals', *Administrative Science Quarterly*, Vol 15, 1970, 271–281

14 HACKMAN J R and LAWLER E E, 'Employee Reactions to Job Characteristics', *Journal of Applied Psychology*, Vol 55, 1971, 259–286

15 LAWLER E E, 'Job Design and Employee Motivation', *Personnel Psychology*, Vol 22, 1969, 426–435

16 VROOM V H, *Work and Motivation*, Wiley, New York, 1964

17 MACE C A, *Incentives: Some Experimental Studies*, HMSO, 1935

18 BRYAN J F and LOCKE E A, 'Goal Setting as a Means of Increasing Motivation', *Journal of Applied Psychology*, Vol 51, 1967

19 LOCKE E A, 'Toward a Theory of Task Motivation and Incentives', *Organizational Behaviour and Human*

Performance, Vol 3, 1968, 157–189

20 FRENCH J R P, KAY E and MEYER H H, 'Participation and the Appraisal System', *Human Relations*, Vol 19, 1966, 3–19

21 CARROLL S J and TOSI H L, 'Goal Characteristics and Personality Factors in a Management-by-Objectives Program', *Administrative Science Quarterly*, Vol 15, 1970, 295–305

22 LOCKE *Op cit*

23 LOCKE E A, CARTLEDGE N and KNERR C S, 'Studies of the Relationship between Satisfaction, Goal-setting, and Performance', *Organizational Behaviour and Human Performance*

24 Since writing this, Zander has reported evidence which supports the Goal Difficulty hypothesis among groups of female workers in a slipper factory. See ZANDER A and ARMSTRONG W, 'Working for Group Pride in a Slipper Factory', *Journal of Applied Social Psychology*, Vol 2, 1972, 293–307

25 TANNER and LAWRENCE, *op cit*

26 HACKMAN and LAWLER, *op cit*

27 FORD R N, *Motivation Through Work Itself*, American Management Association, New York, 1969

28 PATCHEN M, *Participation, Achievement and Involvement on the Job*, Prentice-Hall, Englewood Cliffs, New Jersey, 1970

29 HACKMAN and LAWLER, *op cit*

30 EMERY, *op cit*

31 WYATT, FRASER and STOCK, *op cit*

32 GULOWSEN J, 'A Measure of Work Group Autonomy', *Design of Jobs*, ed Davis L E and Taylor J C, Penguin, 1972

33 ZANDER A, *Motives and Goals in Groups*, Academic Press, New York, 1971

34 RICE A K, *Productivity and Social Organization: the Ahmedabad Experiment*, Tavistock Publications, London, 1958

35 MILLER E J, 'Technology, Territory and Time: the Internal Differentiation of Complex Production Systems', *Human Relations*, Vol 12, 1959, 243–272

CHAPTER FOUR

FORMS OF JOB DESIGN

Job design is essentially a process of allocating task functions among organizational roles. (As we have noted, task functions take the form of planning, executing and controlling.) It implies the idea of 'choice' since there are many different ways of dividing the organization's task and allocating the various functions among organization members.[1]

A key factor in the division-of-work process is the nature of the task itself, and particularly the extent to which it is well-defined and predictable. Well-defined, predictable tasks enable both means and outcomes to be *programmed*, that is, specified with a high degree of precision. Ill-definable, unpredictable tasks necessarily lead to some equivocation with regard to both means and outcomes so that their task operations assume an *unprogrammed* form.[2] Programmed task roles tend to be narrow in function and limited in content; they require little or no recurrent planning and, since there is little intrinsic variance in the task, little control. They are characteristically executive in function and tend to be limited in variety, discretion and contribution. Jobs within a programmed work system pose obvious problems for job enlargement since they have little potential for adding functions other than executive ones (unless it is possible for them to absorb tasks from a contiguous non-programmed system). Unprogrammed roles, in contrast, are varied in function and relatively rich in content. As well as being executive, they invariably include both plan and control functions. Motivationally, they provide conditions conducive to variety, discretion and contribution.

Technology can also determine the form of job design. Woodward (1965) has shown that individual jobs in unit and process production systems encompass planning, executive and control functions together,[3] while in mass and batch production systems managerial and supervisory jobs cover plan—control functions and subordinate roles are almost entirely executive. Level of mechanization can be an important factor. For example, where job performance depends directly on human power (as in assembly tasks), the addition of non-executive functions such as planning may divert the operator from essential manufacturing activity. This would be particularly problematical where productivity norms are emphasized. The addition of varied functions to the job is more practicable where the worker does not contribute directly and continuously to the manufacturing process, as in automated process plants where enlargements of semi-skilled jobs have been effected through the addition of maintenance tasks.

Management values and cognitive styles can determine job design. An organizational logic of cost and efficiency will lead to a different design of work than will an organizational logic of motivation and satisfaction through stimulating job content. Good job design also depends on imagination: the ability to see beyond the limitations of the immediate stiuation.

Where imagination is short, attempts at job design are proportionally limited.

Union and employee attitudes are further relevant factors. Problems of inter-job demarcations can severely limit job design. Even where employees can see that enlargement promises a more satisfying work experience, they may withhold or limit their commitment if their relationship with management is marked by distrust. For example, Paul and Robertson (1970) report on an enlargement of process operating jobs in an Imperial Chemical Industries plant: 'Great difficulty was experienced initially in introducing the fourth change, that each operator should be responsible for two specific plant efficiencies. At that particular time, there was bad feeling in the plant due to difficulties over holidays; the calculations needed for working out the efficiencies were interpreted as an extra chore rather than an attempt to give the men some real control over plant operation.'[4]

The foregoing factors, singly or severally, help to explain why job designs differ so much. Many designs are unnecessarily limited, building around a few convenient job features. Few designs are truly comprehensive.

Designs with limitations

In practice most job enlargement programmes fall far short of the maximum motivation ideal (see chapter 3), being limited largely to variety, means discretion and contribution. This is especially evident in the enlargement of low-skilled industrial jobs as Conant and Kilbridge's (1965) well documented account of an enlargement programme in a factory manufacturing washing machines illustrates.[5] The programme consisted of transferring assembly work from cumulative assembly lines to single work stations where one operator assembled a complete sub-assembly (such as, a water pump). The essential changes were: an increase in the number of tasks performed by one operator (*variety*); the addition of discretion for work pace, work methods, and quality (*means discretion*); and making up a bigger part of the total product (*contribution*). The reasons for the non-inclusion of Skill discretion and goal characteristics are easy to infer. The programmed nature of manufacture by assembly necessarily precludes any possibility of introducing problem-solving, which is the source of skill discretion. Nor is it likely that skill discretion can be introduced by adding boundary jobs that permit problem-solving since this would direct the operator from essential manufacturing activity.

The neglect of goal characteristics follows an implicit assumption of much job enlargement thinking, namely that allocation to the employee of responsibility for work goals (realized in this study by the abolition of line pacing) will automatically lead to higher performance levels. As we have argued, this condition will invariably lead the employee to give priority to quality goals. This receives some support from the enlarged washing appliance jobs, for Conant and Kilbridge report an average decrease in rejects from 2.9 per cent to 1.4 per cent *and* a small decrease in output from 138 per cent to 126 per cent.

Many job enlargements are also somewhat limited in the extent of their augmented features. Whatever motivational gains they make arise largely by comparison with frustratingly meagre pre-enlarged job content. Conant and Kilbridge, for example, report that among the most preferred features of the enlarged jobs they studied were: the freedom to move about on the job; control over quality; opportunity to make complete sub-assembly; and more variety in the job. These seem to reflect expressions of relief rather than of authentic commitment. A similar picture emerges from Cotgrove, Dunham and Vamplew's (1971) recent account of job enlargement in an ICI nylon spinning plant: 'The gains were real. But they were also limited. The main result was the reduction in boredom rather than any major increase in the intrinsic interest in the job'.[6]

Technological constraints on enlargement are most clearly seen on motor vehicle assembly lines. It has long been assumed that the traditional assembly methods of vehicle manufacture will not yield much to enlargement attempts. Objectively this may be so, but even small changes in a highly routine, line-paced job may significantly benefit both employee and performance. Saab-Scania, the Swedish vehicle manufacturer, for example, has enlarged certain chassis assembly jobs by introducing more variety and means discretion as discussed by Norstedt and Aguren.[7] Specifically, the groups of workers have discretion over quality and rotate between the different work tasks. Though small in themselves, the job changes appear to have contributed to increased performance (decrease in unplanned stoppages on line, improved quality), reduced personnel turnover and absenteeism, and increased satisfaction.

In extreme cases, enlargement may not at all enhance

the motivational worth of the job. Davis and Werling (1960), for example, describe a *seemingly* extensive enlargement of distribution workers' jobs in a US chemicals plant.[8] The enlargement was away from the single-function operation of packing a single product into a container to a multi-function operation involving the packing and loading of a variety of products, both dry and liquid. 'Enlargement of these jobs presumed to add a few skills and some diversity of functions and to increase the job scope as to variety of products handled and as to responsibility for completion and inspection. In spite of the increased content, distribution workers felt the jobs lacked meaning and did not permit self-control'. Davis and Werling raise the question 'as to whether sufficient enlargement [had] been introduced to satisfy management's original objectives and workers' needs.'

Designs that compensate

A way of overcoming the limitations imposed on enlargement by inherently routine work is to assimilate other functions from related work systems (provided that this does not interfere with desired performance levels, as noted above). Often this form of enlargement consists of adding functions which do not contribute directly to primary task performance but which are ancillary or supportive in nature.

Davis (1971) has described the creation of new jobs in a Norwegian automated fertilizer plant which illustrates the compensation principle:

'The engineers had designed the plant so that the work to be done (monitoring, diagnosing, and adjusting, there

77

being no physical work done in the plant other than maintenance) would be carried out in three monitoring or control rooms, in front of control panels. The equipment was so sophisticated that it required only one man in each control room. For three work shifts, this would have required nine men . . . the research team wished to avoid a situation in which people would work in isolation. But to put two men in a control room would have been economically inefficient. Therefore, totally new jobs were created by combining the maintenance and control functions. As the completed plant now operates, at least two men are based in each control room, alternately leaving it to perform maintenance tasks. They support each other, and the new job design also brings feed-back from the plant by means other than the instruments on the control panels.'[9]

Paul and Robertson (1970) report several enlargements which include examples of compensatory design.[10] For example, design engineers became involved in the selection and placing of drawing office staff; senior laboratory technicians 'were given the authority to hire labour against agreed manning targets'. In each of these cases, the added functions were ancillary to the primary tasks of those involved.

Designs with 'own' and induced pressures

While current interest in job design is based mainly on increasing job satisfaction, managers hope that enlargement will also result in increased performance. But we have seen from chapter 3 that goal characteristics (goal clarity and difficulty levels) must be emphasized if high productivity is desired. This emphasis will normally be expressed in terms of clear organizational expectations of required performance standards and feedback on performance levels. In this way, the organization structures both clarity and difficulty levels of employee goals. Such externally generated pressures are called 'induced' pressures to distinguish them from 'own' pressures which have their source in the job itself and over which the employee has direct control. 'Own' pressures reflect the common-sense and scientifically-validated observation that people feel more responsible for decisions which they themselves make and are more committed to the actions which follow than is the case where they are induced to carry out someone else's decisions.[11]

However, given discretion over his own goals, the employee will normally emphasize the quality rather than the quantity of his performance. (Presumably because quality is the feature which most clearly defines a 'good worker'.) Additional 'induced' pressures are often necessary to ensure that quantity goals are achieved. Collaborative target-setting between superior and subordinate is a good example of 'induced' pressure.[12]

Robert Ford's (1969) account of the enlargement of computer clerks' jobs in the American Telegraph and Telephone Company well illustrates how 'own' and 'induced' pressures operate as motivators.[13] Along with a number of changes intended to increase the clerks' levels of means discretion, the following performance criteria were emphasized:

1 Each clerk was given definite assignments and completion dates. With these in mind, clerks scheduled their own work to meet job requirements

2 Each clerk helped set her own deadline dates. (Presumably she did this with a superior in 'participative goal-setting' sessions)
3 Each clerk was given direct feedback on output errors and was to make necessary corrections. (Previously this was done by an assignment clerk or verifier)

Not surprisingly, quality *and* quantity performance gains were observed. Ford reports similar results for other enlarged clerical jobs.

Designs that cope with variance

Many jobs are characterized by disturbances and uncertainties—variance—that hinder goal attainment. Dealing with such conditions requires jobs high on both forms of discretion, ie, means and skill. Probably the best known, and certainly the best documented, example of job design for coping with variance is that reported by Trist and his colleagues (1963) at the Tavistock Institute of Human Relations in a study of the effects of technological change in a British coal mine.[14] The exact nature of variance at the coal face is described as follows:

'The underground situation can vary greatly from one face to another and from one type of system to another, but common to all is the absence of fixed and consistent conditions in the physical environment. The complex of factors affecting work at the coal face is of the kind that would confront a factory if productive machinery had to be moved and re-set every day; if every operator had to contend with constant minor changes in the material he was working on; and, at the same time, look to keeping the walls and roof of his work area supported because they were imminently liable to collapse; if all supplies had to be brought in and products removed through two narrow passages; and if, despite the absence of uniform working conditions, supervisors could visit the operators only occasionally throughout one shift. Unlike the factory situation, where a high degree of control can be exercised over the production process since working conditions can be maintained in a passive and constant state, in the underground situation the threat of instability from the environment makes the production task much more liable to disorganization.'

The pre-change method of coal-getting involved small groups of miners, usually two or three, working closely together. These groups enjoyed a high level of discretion in that control over the task was wholly internal to the group (miners even chose their own work mates) and the only contact the group had with external colliery management was in contracting to work a particular wall of the coal face. Within these small undifferentiated groups each coal miner was called on to execute a variety of tasks, often substituting for his mate. In addition, group members experienced a sense of contribution inasmuch as they completed the entire cycle of operations necessary to hew a given face.

The technological innovation consisted of substituting mechanical coal-cutters and conveyors for the old hand-got methods, thus transforming the production technology to a type characteristic of mass production methods. Instead of working a series of short faces, a costly method of coal extraction, mechanization made it possible to work a single long wall. The new long-wall method demanded a different form of individual and group working than prevailed with the hand-got method. The production unit was organized around the cycle group of about 40 men who had to extract about 200 tons of coal per cycle. A cycle extended over 24 hours, made up of three shifts of $7\frac{1}{2}$ hours each. The allocation of workmen to each shift was approximately 10 to the first 'cutting' shift, 10 to the second 'ripping' shift, and 20 to the third 'filling' shift. Within each of the shifts, individuals were restricted to narrowly defined work roles in contrast to the task variety inherent in the hand-got method. However, the real lack of integration between the miners and the technology lay in the high degree of interdependence between the tasks throughout the entire cycle. Operational problems experienced at one stage of the process were carried forward to later stages, and because the inflexible nature of the production process did not permit the carrying on of later tasks while hold-ups were being dealt with, the system was necessarily highly sensitive to disruption both at the production and social-psychological levels. And, since discretion was no longer functionally vested in the working group, the miners experienced a sense of impotence and frustration in the face of the complex and inflexible technological system. Consequently they developed various defensive manoeuvres: a norm of low productivity as a means of reducing disturbances which were beyond their control; the creation of small informal groups whose major obligations were to themselves and not to the cycle system as a whole; individual competition for the more workable parts of the coal face and for special favours from co-workers whose own work could help or hinder one's particular task area. Absenteeism, as a means of withdrawal, also became widespread.

Trist and his colleagues underline the importance of skill discretion (which they call 'conceptual Skill') under the new technology, particularly in using knowledge to anticipate future contingencies:

'Even with the most intricate machine a good deal of judgment must be exercised by its operator to ensure the best results. . . . There is wide scope for the use of discretion. This centres on the regulatory processes, because, if a machine is held up or works too far below capacity, the losses are altogether more serious than in lower register systems. A key regulatory function is anticipation, which covers not only preventive main-tenance of machinery and face conditions, but enters into the way all work is done in relation to other groups. When mechanical or geological difficulties call for rechannelling of effort or redepolyment of men, the speed and efficiency with which counteraction is taken makes a significant difference to the duration of lost time. A high degree of anticipation coupled with early and effective counter-action maintain optimum machine use . . . If in lower register systems the use of discretion is in no small measure a matter of how much physical effort is applied, under full mechanization it has a different quality, being much more a question of understanding the system as a whole and reacting with perspicacity to its demands.'[15]

In a later series of studies in other coalfields, the Tavistock researchers were able to compare the efficiency of the conventional longwall method of extraction with another method, the *composite* longwall method, which, while still employing the new technology described above, utilized some of the design features of the older manual methods, especially discretion for means and skill. In the composite method, men arriving for a new shift take up the cycle point left by the previous shift. When their main task is completed, they then carry on with the next task, whether or not this happens to be part of the current cycle or begins another cycle. That is, unlike the men in conventional longwalling, they act somewhat independently of the strict cycle process determined by the technology. The composite method also provides a greater variety of skills for the individual worker, thus making for greater job satisfaction. Composite teams are also self-selected and are paid on a common paynote in which all group members share equally. Tables 1 and 2 show the relative efficiency levels of teams working the same technology and coal seam but with different job designs.

TABLE 1

Productivity indexes for two different production systems in coal mining

| Index | Longwall | |
	Conventional	Composite
Productivity (% of coal face potential)	78	95
State of cycle progress:		
In advance	0	22
Normal	31	73
Behind	69	5

TABLE 2

Absence rates (% of possible shifts) for two different production systems in coal mining

Reasons for absence	Longwall	
	Conventional	Composite
No reason given	4.3	0.4
Sickness and other	8.9	4.6
Accident	6.8	3.2
Total	20.0	8.2

We noted in chapter 3 that group tasks, compared with individual tasks, have an additional design problem in that they are made up of interdependent sub-tasks which require coordination. In highly variable tasks, interdependence tends to be reciprocal, with group members contributing reciprocally to each other's activities, and coordination tends to be by mutual adjustment, with group members adjusting their activities to each other on the basis of variable task demands. We also noted another requirement of variable group tasks, namely that individual group members should be capable of carrying out a variety of functions. This facilitates reciprocation and co-ordination of activities within the group and contributes significantly to its effectiveness.

Evidence in support of this design is found in the Tavistock study. Two composite longwall panels (a panel is a complete length of coal face) having identical conditions were compared. In time the groups developed different ways of organizing themselves. The essential differences centred around the multi-skilled nature of individual roles:

No 1 Panel	*No 2 Panel*
Two face teams, each with responsibility for manning the three shifts on its particular face (ie, complete panel divided into 2 faces)	Two main shift groups, each responsible for whole panel
Men work at one main task	Men rotate tasks systematically
Each task and work place tied to a particular man	Tasks and work places not tied to individuals
Not custom for men to move from one work group to another	Men move freely from one work group to another

No 2 panel was superior in terms of performance, satisfaction and absenteeism:

'This . . . comparison leads to the general conclusion that, for workers carrying out a primary task comprising interdependent component activities interchangeable between group members, the (varied) form of organization has inherent characteristics more conducive to productive effectiveness, work satisfaction, and social health than that based on separately treated single task groups.'[16]

A more recent example of design for variance control

is reported by Engelstad (1972) in the Hunsfoss (Norway) pulp and papermill.[17] Papermaking is a succession of processes in which fibrous raw material is pulped to a suspension of fibres in water and then formed into a continuous 'web' or 'band' of paper. The successional nature of the process means that uncontrolled variations are transmitted along the various production stages. In the Hunsfoss mill, the sources of variance derived from the nature of the raw materials and the technical equipment.

In the pre-change situation, operators worked at one main task and were 'tied' to one particular work place. In addition '. . . the foreman had developed the practice of being constantly on the move as a troubleshooter within the department; he would then do most of the unpredictable tasks that the operators were reluctant to carry out without special compensations, perceiving such tasks as falling outside their own strictly defined jobs . . . By filling in for their subordinates, the managers and foremen were subtly redefining their own jobs in a way that reinforced the tendencies of the men on the shop floor not to show more initiative than was demanded by the traditional job design.' To overcome this, increased discretion for both means and skill was introduced to the extent that:

1 The men as a group took more responsibility for the operation of the department as a whole
2 They were encouraged and helped to increase their understanding and control of the various processes. Operators were trained as far as was possible in all tasks within the department

Increased work interest was observed among operators,

87

and substantial improvements in plant performance were recorded. However, since goal characteristics (particularly clarity of quality and quantity standards) were also emphasized in this study, it is likely that the performance increases flowed directly from a keener appreciation of goal requirements, supported by a climate of greater personal and group control.

Some comprehensive designs

The ideal aim of job design programmes should be to create jobs that amply represent all four characteristics of variety, discretion (both for means and skill), contribution and goal characteristics so that optimal performance and satisfaction requirements can be achieved simultaneously. We have seen that, for a number of reasons, this ideal is rarely observed.

Professional and managerial jobs probably have the most potential for such comprehensive enlargements. As an example, Paul and Robertson (1970) report an enlargement of Experimental Officers' (EOs) jobs in an ICI research and development department.[18] These staff implemented experimental programmes devised by graduate scientists. The enlargement was an attempt to raise EOs' morale in a situation where they felt that, among other things, 'their technical ability and experience was being wasted by graduates, refusal to delegate anything except routine work.' The main job changes concerned skill discretion (planning projects and experiments, freedom to research own ideas, devising and implementing training programmes for junior staff), means discretion (responsibility for requisitioning materials and equipment, ordering services such as maintenance, requesting experimental analysis, responsibility for staff assessment, etc), contribution (personal preparation and authorizing of final reports on research projects for which responsible), and goal characteristics (EOs contributed to target setting). Evidence of increased quantity and quality in performance was noted; no satisfaction increases were observed but this may have been due to imperfect research methodology.

A successful instance of comprehensive design with low-skilled jobs is reported by Weed (1971) at Texas Instruments.[19] Prior to 1967, Texas Instruments' cleaning and janitorial services (at its Dallas, Texas plant) were carried out by an outside contractor. The company evaluated the plant as only 65 per cent clean. The contractor's ability to do the job well was cramped by a quarterly turnover rate of 100 per cent. Instead of using the contractors' services, the company established its own cleaning teams and designed their jobs with the following criteria in mind:

1 Teams were encouraged to identify problems and to solve them creatively (skill discretion)
2 They were assigned overall job responsibilities with the method of meeting these responsibilities left to them (means discretion)
3 They developed their own work schedules and operating procedures as teams (means discretion)
4 They contributed to goal setting for their own jobs (goal characteristics)
5 Individuals were assigned specific areas of cleaning responsibility (contribution)

Results were:

1 The cleanliness rating improved from 65 per cent to 85 per cent.

2 Number of personnel required for cleaning dropped from 120 to 71

3 Quarterly turnover dropped from 100 per cent to 9.8 per cent

Probably the most extensive instance of job design yet reported developed from the establishment by General Foods Corporation of a new plant for manufacturing pet foods in Topeka (Kansas).[26] Existing plants in the company, though continuous process, suffered from overt employee disaffection due apparently to the routine and non-involving nature of the technology. The major task features incorporated in the new plant were:

1 *Means discretion* at both individual and group levels. Discretionary areas included:

(i) Main production processes, eg, unloading and storage of raw materials, drawing materials, drawing ingredients from storage, mixing, etc

(ii) Coping with manufacturing problems that occurred within or between the teams' areas of responsibilities

(iii) Temporarily redistributing tasks to cover for absent employees

(iv) Compelling employees who do not meet team standards (eg, regarding absence or helping others in need)

    (v) Selecting team operators to serve on plant-wide committees or project teams

    (vi) Screening and selecting employees to replace departing operators

2 *Skill discretion:* All tasks designed 'to include functions requiring higher-order human abilities' such as planning and diagnosing mechanical or process problems

3 *Contribution through performing 'whole' task.* Functional specialization was avoided. 'Activities typically performed by maintenance, quality control, custodial, industrial engineering, and personnel units are built into an operating team's responsibilities. For example, each team member maintains (most of) the equipment he operates and housekeeps the area in which he works. Each team has responsibility for performing quality tests and ensuring quality standards. In addition, team members perform what is normally a personnel function when they screen job applicants'

In addition, among a number of organizational innovations which helped to support the above design are the following:

1 *Job mobility and rewards for learning:* Pay increases depended on the employee mastering an increasing proportion of jobs first in the team and then in the wider plant. 'In effect, team members are paid for learning more and more aspects of the total manufacturing system. Because there are no limits on the number of operators that can qualify for higher pay brackets, employees are encouraged to teach each

91

other'

2 *Facilitative leadership:* Team leaders were mainly responsible for team development and group decision-making, in contrast to the company's traditional conception of supervision as being the planning and control of subordinates' performance

3 *Plant-wide equality:* Social and status differences in the plant as a whole were minimized through 'an open parking lot, a single entrance for both the office and plant, and a common decor throughout the reception area, offices, locker rooms, and cafeteria'

Various criteria of success are reported including high performance measures (especially quality), low absenteeism as well as evidence of high commitment and satisfaction.

Addenda

Two further points. Whatever form job design takes, it should be augmented by *developmental design* and *organizational supports*.

Developmental design describes the continuous and progressive enlargement of jobs in order to meet people's needs for continued growth and learning. Once the employee has successfully mastered added challenges and responsibilities he becomes restless for more. Job design should not be seen as a solitary, once-for-all step but rather as a cumulative process which ends only when the individual feels he has reached, but not exceeded, the limits of his growth capacity.

Organizational supports refer quite simply to those organizational conditions which help to maintain and aid the development of job designs. They may take the form of managerial and employee commitment to the idea of job enlargement itself or structural supports, such as the availability of correct and adequate information for decision-making. At a more basic level, job design will not 'take' if the everyday hygiene factors (eg, pay, supervision) are a cause of dissatisfaction.

REFERENCES

1 SIMON H A, *Administrative Behavior*. Macmillan Co. New York, 1951

2 MARCH J and SIMON H A, *Organizations*, Wiley, New York, 1958

3 WOODWARD J, *Industrial Organization: Theory and Practice*, Oxford University Press, 1965

4 PAUL W J and ROBERTSON K B, *Job Enrichment and Employee Motivation*, Gower Press, London, 1970

5 CONANT E H and KILBRIDGE M D, 'An Interdisciplinary Analysis of Job Enlargement: Technology, Costs and Behavioral Implications', *Industrial and Labor Relations Review*, Vol 18, 1965, 377–395

6 COTGROVE S, DUNHAM J and VAMPLEW C, *The Nylon Spinners*, George Allen and Unwin, 1971

7 NORSTEDT J-P and AGUREN S, *The Saab-Scania Report*, Swedish Employers' Confederation, Stockholm, 1973

8 DAVIS L E and WERLING R, 'Job Design Factors', *Occupational Psychology*, Vol 34, 109–132, 1960

9 DAVIS L E, 'Readying the Unready: Post-industrial Jobs', *California Management Review*, Vol 13, 1971, 27–36

10 Paul W J and Robertson K B, *op cit*

11 For a theoretical discussion of this point, see
    Kiesler C, *The Psychology of Commitment*, Academic
    Press, New York, 1971

12 McGregor D, *The Human Side of Enterprise*,
    McGraw-Hill, New York, 1960. See especially
    Chapter 5

13 Ford R N, *Motivation Through the Work Itself*,
    American Management Association, New York,
    1969

14 Trist E L, Higgin G W, Murray H and Pollock
    A B, *Organizational Choice: Capabilities of Groups at
    the Coal Face Under Changing Technologies*, Tavistock
    Publications, London, 1963

15, 16 Trist, Higgin, Murray and Pollock, *op cit*

17 Engelstad P H, 'Socio-Technical Approach to
    Problems of Process Control', Chapter 23 in
    Davis L E and Taylor J C (eds), *Design of Jobs*,
    Penguin Books, 1972

18 Paul and Robertson, *op cit*

19 Weed E D, 'Job Enrichment "Cleans Up" at
    Texas Instruments', Chapter 4 in Maher J R
    (ed), *New Perspectives in Job Enrichment*, Van
    Nostrand Reinhold, New York, 1971

20 Walton R E, 'How to Counter Alienation in the
    Plant', *Harvard Business Review*, Nov-Dec 1972,
    70–81

JOB DESIGN AS PLANNED CHANGE

As with other forms of organizational development, the success of job design depends very much on the extent and quality of its prior planning and preparation. Prior mapping of the change process includes identifying the required changes in job content as well as developing the right relationship with the members of the target system. This latter point is needed to palliate the 'technocratic bias' of change programmes, ie, 'the belief that once you have worked out the general ideas in the form of a change programme, then the client can carry it out with dispatch. The technocratic bias rarely, in fact, works without some form of collaboration between the change-agent and the client. Change often depends more on interpersonal than on rational skills'.[1]

It is helpful if management's motives for job design are made explicit at the very beginning. If job design is used simply to cure a local ill (such as high labour turnover), its potential for enhancing overall organizational effectiveness may be overlooked. If it is seen essentially as a tool for increasing productivity or utilizing labour more efficiently, it may be viewed by employees as a manipulative device and not as a means for enriching their work experience. In other words, the reasons behind the job design, together with its implications, should be thoroughly thought through before being translated into action.

An important ground rule in planned organizational change is to approach the change process not just as a problem-solving exercise but as a *learning process*. The complex nature of many job designs means that unforeseen problems often emerge and consequently mistakes are often made. These have to be accepted as natural features of planned change. Viewed in this way, problems and mistakes become potential sources of learning which can contribute to the success of the change rather than factors which simply impede progress towards a solution.

Selecting a site

Choice of an appropriate site for job redesign is an obvious initial consideration. Where enlargement is being attempted for the first time, the chosen jobs should be those which are likely to have a real impact on the organization's effectiveness; that is, they should be jobs that contribute directly to key operational goals rather than jobs which are mainly supportive in function (eg, catering, security). There are two reasons for this. Firstly, successful results in key work areas are likely to have far greater credibility than results from supportive work areas; this is especially important where the organization is hoping for the general commitment of managers and employees to an extensive programme of redesign. Secondly, redesign in key operating areas, particularly through delegation of discretion, helps to free key managerial functions from day-to-day supervisory responsibilities, thus permitting managers to spend more time on long-term planning and development.

Choice of an initial site should also include the commitment of site management and employees. Without this commitment, the redesign will have little or no success. Management in particular should also be committed enough to tolerate the temporary risks and setbacks sometimes associated with redesign.

The organizational nature of the chosen site should be examined in relation to the rest of the organization. New values and behaviour brought about by job enlargement should be congruent with values and behaviour in other (especially contiguous) parts of the system. Whyte (1955) reports a case where a successful enlargement in one section of a company had disagreeable repercussions in other departments.[2] The company manufactured wooden toys; one part of the process involved spraying paint on the partially assembled toys and hanging them on moving hooks which carried them through a drying oven. This operation, staffed entirely by girls, was plagued by absenteeism, high turnover and low morale. Complaints centred round the unreasonably fast speed of the moving hooks, over which the girls had no control. The job change consisted essentially of giving the girls full control over the speed of the hooks. Production increased and within three weeks the group was operating at 30 per cent to 50 per cent above the original, time-studied performance levels. The girls' earnings became correspondingly higher than expected. As well as their basic pay, they earned a considerable piece-rate bonus which made their wages more than those of many skilled workers in other parts of the plant. Management was pressed to remove this inequity and it did this by returning the job to its original design. Predictably' production dropped and within a month all but two of the eight girls in the group had quit.

Such unintended effects of job enlargement can be circumvented by 'sheltering' the experimental site from normal working pressures and demands. Davis and Trist (1972) describe the use of the 'sheltered experiment' in a Canadian continuous casting plant: 'The 'experiment' lasted 12 months and was sheltered from management rules and union contract so that both parties could see the concrete outcome after the men in the crew had learned the tasks in their new roles and had learned to operate the new technology'.[3]

Generating ideas for changing job content

A prerequisite for developing enlarged jobs is a sound knowledge, first of motivational theory, particularly intrinsic motivation (see chapter 2), and, secondly, the specific characteristics of job content that activate and satisfy the intrinsic needs (see chapter 3).

The next step is to translate the theoretical knowledge into practical suggestions for specific jobs. This requires the participation of personnel (eg, managers, supervisors) who have a good grasp of the theory as well as an intimate knowledge of the jobs to be changed. However, a commonly experienced problem is that such people, though versed in theory and practice, often have difficulty in producing ideas suitable for good design. This may be because, as Herzberg suggests,

99

they have been conditioned into thinking that the content of jobs is sacrosanct and/or they cling to outmoded motivational beliefs (by emphasizing hygiene factors for example) which are irrelevant to the specific problem of enhancing performance and satisfaction through the *content* of the job.[4] Brainstorming (an ideas-producing process with explicit rules forbidding criticism, ridicule and inflexibility) is recommended in order to get round this difficulty. The list of change items produced through brainstorming is then examined and all hygiene factors (those relating to security, wages, status, social factors and company policy) are deleted. The remaining items should relate only to the *content* of the jobs being changed. The next step is to classify the items according to the dimensions of the job framework described in chapter 3, ie, variety, discretion, contribution and goal characteristics. This step serves to check how well the brainstormed list of job-content items covers the ideal motivational framework. If some dimensions are not covered, further suggestions can be sought. (Remember that variety is not a true motivator and therefore need not be emphasized.) The final step should be to integrate the classified list of job-content items into a meaningful plan—execute—control module.

In summary, the above process consists of:

1 Brainstorming a list of items for improving motivation and satisfaction

2 Delete hygiene factors from list

3 Classify remaining job-content items in terms of variety, means and skill discretion, contribution, and goal characteristics. (Remember that variety is

not a true motivator)

4 If some of the above job dimensions are not represented in the list, seek further suggestions

5 Integrate the listed items into a meaningful plan— execute—control module

My own experience of job design leads me to believe that the brainstorming step can often be quite safely abandoned *provided* the designers are highly committed to change and are very knowledgeable with regard to job design theory and the particular jobs being changed. But brainstorming does have the advantage of ensuring a comprehensive coverage of possible job-content items.

Other and more detailed approaches to the process of generating ideas for job improvement can be found in Herzberg, Ford and Myers.[5][6][7]

The role of employees in implementing job change

Whether employees should participate in job-design implementation is variously disputed. Herzberg (1968), for example, claims that employee involvement 'contaminates the [job design] process with human relations *hygiene* and, more specifically, gives them only a *sense* of making a contribution. The job is to be changed, and it is the content that will produce the motivation, not attitudes about being involved or the challenge inherent in setting up a job'.[8] This view represents a *tactical* approach to job design, in other words, it focuses on job design as an organizational tool for improving performance and satisfaction. It contrasts with the *organic* approach which sees job design as one of several means for developing the capacities of organizational members (especially lower-level members). The organic approach views employee participation in job design as an equally necessary experience for growth.

The tactical and organic approaches have been aptly caricatured as, respectively, tell/sell and consult/participate.[9] Table 3 presents the definitive features of each approach.

TABLE 3

Sources of Proposals for Job Redesign

by Roger Maitland*

Introduction

The process by which a decision is reached is often as important as the nature of the decision itself. Two processes for reaching decisions about job redesign are in common use: the consult/participate approach, in which job incumbents say what is wrong with their own jobs and suggest ways in which they could be changed; and the tell/sell approach, in which the primary sources for job analysis and changes in job design are not the workers themselves but their supervisors and higher management. Each approach takes into account the feelings of the work force but by different means and with different ends in view. The consult/participate approach administers a questionnaire before any changes are introduced in order to see whether the job incumbents regard job enrichment as psychologically applicable. The tell/sell approach

*I am grateful to Roger Maitland, Consultant, Manpower Planning, Research and Statistics Section, British Steel Corporation, for allowing me to use his previously unpublished material.

administers an attitude survey both before and after changes are introduced in order to see whether job enrichment has been psychologically successful with the job incumbents. Each approach has its own advantages and disadvantages, expressed as arguments for and against participation, with relation to six basic problems:

1 The problem of stimulating suggestions

tell/sell

Employees cannot make suggestions for job redesign because:

(a) they are not sufficiently intelligent

(b) they have a limited awareness of their own potential for development because they have never been given the opportunity to explore it

(c) they have a limited awareness of

consult/participate

Employees can make suggestions for job redesign because:

(a) the capacity to exercise a relatively high degree of imagination and creativity is widely, not narrowly, distributed in the population

(b) symptoms of false consciousness are not identical with manifestations of basic human nature

(c) symptoms of adaptation are not

how their jobs could be developed because their experiences within them have estranged them from the intellectual potentialities of the labour process

(d) they have been encouraged by existing reward systems to monetise all their motives

(e) they have been constrained by collective bargaining procedures to think of improvements purely in maintenance terms

2 The problem of getting suggestions

tell/sell

Employees will not make suggestions for job design because:

(a) past experience has shown them synonymous with ignorance of preferred alternatives

(d) managers are just as likely to concentrate on 'hygiene' factors as workers

(e) workers are capable of distinguishing the operating context from the negotiating context as well as managers

consult/participate

Employees will make suggestions for job redesign if:

(a) they are assured by management of

that management are not willing
to make such changes

(b) political constraints operate against
workers making suggestions due to
their fears of being branded
troublemakers, whereas these
constraints are far less strongly felt
at higher levels in the enterprise

(c) workers do not feel that it is their
job to suggest changes and they
resent any managerial attempts to
pass the buck

(d) workers do not want to help
management solve problems because
they do not share the same
commitment to the same objectives

That is, changes in behaviour are
necessary before changes in attitudes are

their commitment to job enrichment

(b) they are allowed to brainstorm ideas
in a situation free from the fear of
reprimand or reprisal

(c) they are convinced that they have a
valuable contribution to make

(d) they are shown that it is in their own
interests to increase the size of the
cake and that to do so will not
interfere with the traditional methods
for deciding how it will be divided up

That is, changes in attitudes are necessary
before changes in behaviour are possible.

possible. Values will not change without a change in social structure; and although a readiness to make the system work can be elicited, jobs must be changed first.
A commitment to organizational objectives is a product of social concern, and social concern is a product of technical proficiency

A change in social structure will not come about without a change in values; and although jobs can be changed, a readiness to make the system work must be established first. Technical proficiency is a product of social concern, and social concern is a product of commitment to organizational objectives

3   The problem of getting practical suggestions

tell/sell

Managers have the best idea of whether suggestions are practical or not because:
(a) they have the most comprehensive knowledge of the other parts of the system where suggestions will have repercussions

(b) they are aware of the relative advantages and disadvantages of a

consult/participate

Workers have the best idea of whether suggestions are practical or not because:
(a) they have the most intimate knowledge of what particular tasks entail

(b) they are aware of the relative advantages and disadvantages of a particular suggestion for the company as a whole

particular suggestion for a job incumbent

4 The problem of getting relevant suggestions

tell/sell

Managers will have the best idea of whether suggestions are relevant or not to workers' needs and abilities because:

(a) needs are not a given in the work situation but a variable. Jobs do not merely satisfy or frustrate needs, they modify them. Changes in jobs will therefore lead to changes in needs

(b) democracy is not a question of counting up opinions but of liberating energies and opening horizons to the widest human limits

(c) jobs will not be enriched without

consult/participate

Workers will have the best idea of whether suggestions are relevant or not to their needs and abilities because:

(a) needs vary in the degree to which they are shared by individuals

(b) needs vary in the extent to which they are important to individuals

(c) abilities vary in the degree to which

giving the incumbents the requisite training necessary to meet the new demands. Abilities are not given as constraints but are variables which can be developed

(d) there is no reason why people who need or value something should be able to identify, express or articulate it

they are possessed by individuals

(b) abilities vary in the extent to which they are valued by individuals

5 The problem of getting acceptable suggestions

tell/sell

If workers are involved in making suggestions they are less likely to accept their implementation because:

(a) the shame involved in seduction, where one is a partner to one's own downfall, is harder to bear than the

consult/participate

If workers are involved in making suggestions they are more likely to accept their implementation because:

(a) they will be more committed to changes which they themselves helped to engineer martyrdom involved in rape

(b) changes introduced in order to conform with existing capacities are likely to have a relatively shortlived motivational effect

(c) not all suggestions made by workers about their jobs will have been accepted due to external constraints, and involvement without influence will be counterproductive motivationally because expectations will have been raised only to be disappointed

(b) they will be more confident of their ability to cope with the changes because they will not have suggested anything which they regard as beyond their reach

(c) they will be convinced of the integrity of management because they will already have been involved in making decisions which affect their jobs

6 The problem of getting measurable suggestions

tell/sell

If workers are involved in analysing and redesigning jobs, then the results of job

consult/participate

If workers are involved in analysing and redesigning jobs, then the results of job enrichment will be harder to measure because:

(a) some of the results will be the function of a Hawthorne effect, due to the fact that people will realise that they are participating in a special exercise

(b) the exercise will take on the nature of a bargaining process rather than a scientific experiment

(c) some of the results will be self-fulfilling prophecies because workers will be anxious to prove the validity of ideas which they themselves suggested

enrichment will be no harder to measure because:

(a) a Hawthorne effect is unavoidable: to study a Hawthorne effect you need to study people, and if you study people you get a Hawthorne effect

(b) a Hawthorne effect is not necessarily undesirable: changes which are small enough to be hardly noticeable are unlikely to be large enough to be really significant

(c) a Hawthorne effect can be advantageous: the time that it is likely to last for is just long enough to compensate for the initial drop in production which usually takes place in job enrichment experiments

Conclusion

Both approaches have their advantages and disadvantages. A compromise must therefore be reached. We must ensure that suggestions are forthcoming and that these are practical, relevant, acceptable and measurable, but we must also ensure that the mode of implementing job enrichment manifests the spirit of its underlying philosophy.

Some further aspects of implementation

While it is desirable for top management to be committed to job design projects, it is by no means a necessary condition for their success. Local initiatives at departmental or section levels can often generate their own success and serve to stimulate other groups to attempt their own redesign programmes. Beer and Huse (1972) describe just such a process which occurred in the Corning Glass Works (Corning, New York):

'An early example of the development of change leaders in our work with this company was the successful joint effort of an engineer and a supervisor to redesign a hotplate assembly operation which would eliminate an assembly line and give each worker total responsibility for the assembly of a particular product. It resulted in a productivity increase of close to 50 per cent, a drop in rejects from 23 per cent, controllable rejects to close to 1 per cent, and a reduction in absenteeism from about 8 per cent to less than 1 per cent in a few months. Not all the early experiments were successful, but mistakes were treated as part of the experimental learning process.

'As some in the organization changed and moved ahead by trying out new behaviours, others watched and waited but were eventually influenced by the culture. An example of late changers so influenced was the superior of Materials Control, who watched for two years what was going on in the plant but basically disagreed with the concept of OD (organizational development). Then he began to feel pressure to change because his peers were trying new things and he was not. He began by experimenting with enriching his secretary's job and found, in his own words, that "she was doing three times as much, enjoying it more, and giving me more time to manage". When he found that this experiment in managerial behaviour had 'paid off', he began to take a more active interest in OD. His next step was to completely reorganize his department to push decision making down the ladder, to utilize a team approach, and to enrich jobs. He supervised four sections: purchasing, inventory control, plant scheduling and expediting. Reorganization of Materials Control was around product line teams, including the four functions described above. We moved slowly and discussed with him alternative ways of going about the structural change. When he made the change, his subordinates were prepared and ready. The results were clear: In a three-month period of time (with the volume of business remaining steady), the parts shortage list was reduced from 14 IBM pages to less than a page. In other words, although he was a late-changer in terms of the developing culture, his later actions were highly successful.'[10]

The use of local groups also satisfies the need to keep job improvements in 'low profile'. Large-scale programmes instituted by top management may unwittingly create lofty and unrealizable expectations among employees. Organization-wide programmes probably have a greater chance of success when they are based on considerable 'grass roots' experience.

If local designs are to be used as the basis of larger programmes, their didactic value can be increased if they are conducted as experiments which specify and measure the major variables of interest under controlled conditions. Results from controlled experiments may also carry more conviction with other potential users of job design compared with results obtained by less exact methods.

Redesign is also a learning process for employees. They must acquire new knowledge and skills which may, depending on the extent of the redesign, necessitate some formal training. But even without formal training, a climate conducive to learning is needed, and this depends on the appreciation that people need time to master new knowledge and that they can be expected to make mistakes while they are learning. To facilitate the learning process, Herzberg suggests that the constituent elements of the redesign be added one at a time at suitable intervals; one element per week for example.

It is worth noting briefly that 'green field' locations, compared with existing work systems, have greater potential for innovation. This applies not only to the design itself but also to support features in the wider organization, such as those that tend to reduce status differentials and contribute to interpersonal openness.[11]

Such participative systems demand high quality personnel and may therefore benefit from using formal selection methods. King (1971) summarizes the argument for using selection techniques as follows:

'People . . . must be selected for very different kinds of organizational roles than they have previously experienced. This poses an interesting transactional problem. The selection decision makers must obtain an accurate indication of whether or not the candidate is likely to function well in a participative organization. At the same time, prospective employees need accurate information to assist them in deciding whether or not it is advisable for them to join such a new system.'[12]

King describes techniques used to select supervisors and operators who were to man the participative work system in the new General Foods plant described in chapter 4.

Remunerating bigger jobs

The fact that organizational members differ widely in the degree to which they identify with organizational goals has important consequences for remunerating employees who assume more responsibility through redesign. Managers tend to perceive their own careers as being closely congruent with their organization's achievements. In contrast, lower-level employees tend to view their relationship with the organization in contractual terms, based on the exchange of their effort for monetary and other rewards. The latter might therefore be expected to demand financial compensation for assuming bigger jobs, while managers would perhaps regard the increased responsibilities deriving from redesign simply as a means for enhancing their contribution to organizational performance.

Another aspect of this difference is the climate of union-management relationships dominated by a 'distributive bargaining model' which derives from the view that organizational members' inputs and rewards are essentially 'limited resources' and therefore should be equitably allocated.[13] Daniel and McIntosh (1972) have recently described a number of industrial cases where job enlargement was introduced through productivity bargaining.[14] However, in contrast, Paul and Robertson (1970) report a number of enlargements among staff *and* payroll employees of ICI which were not accompanied by demands for higher pay.[15] Similarly, Beer and Huse comment on the redesigns at Corning Glass: '. . . no significant pressures for higher pay have been felt to date'—though they add: 'However, there has been sufficient opportunity for promotion of hourly employees to higher level jobs as the plant has grown'.[16]

Profit-sharing has been suggested as an equitable means of remunerating enlarged jobs. The recent *Work in America* report argues that:

> 'Participation in profits is needed to avoid having workers feel that participative management is merely a refined Tayloristic technique for improving productivity at their expense. The redesign of work tasks through participation will increase productivity, but some experience has indicated that without profit sharing workers may feel that they have been manipulated, and productivity may slip back to former levels. Profit sharing is also the most direct response to the problem of equitable wage increases for employees: the contribution of the worker can be tied directly to his salary increases'.[17]

The report also discusses a number of specific requirements for successful profit-sharing.

Evaluating the success of job design

Like all social experiments and reforms, job design suffers from over-zealous proselytisers and uncritical good intenders. Its literature is suffused with a mythology of success. Exaggerated and even utopian claims are often made for projects involving only a handful of employees whose jobs have undergone but marginal change. There is a sense of *willed* bemusement about the evaluation of many projects which seems unable to appreciate the possibility of failure or deficiency.[18] This seduction has affected behavioural scientists just as much as managers. In this regard, Donald Campbell (1969) has warned us: 'If the political and administrative system has committed itself in advance to the correctness and efficacy of its reforms, it cannot tolerate learning of failure. To be truly scientific we must be able to experiment. We must be able to advocate without that excess of commitment that blinds us to reality testing'.[19]

Scientific evaluation of work-system change depends firstly on reliable measures, and secondly on a methodology for checking the cause-effect relationships between the redesigned job content and the dependent measures.

Typically, dependent measures include performance, satisfaction, absenteeism and turnover indices. Use of these indices ranges from a general appreciation or intuitive 'feel' to an extensive data-collection programme using refined quantitative data.

Common methods for checking the causal relationships between job content changes and dependent measures take two basic forms: *before-after* designs and *control* designs. The before-after design is essentially a 'one-group pretest—posttest design', ie, it subjects one group of employees to experimental changes in job content and evaluates their effects (or non-effects) by comparing the behaviour of the group (usually in comparable time units) before and after the experimental change. Observed differences in behaviour are then attributed to the change. The most obvious criticism of this method is that it cannot be sure that the observed effects are not due to adventitious influences from other parts of the organization.

The control design transcends this limitation by comparing two groups matched in terms of jobs, members' backgrounds, tenure, etc, only one of which is subjected to the experimental job changes. Behaviour differences (if any) between the two groups are more specifically attributable to the job changes than to other possible contaminating factors. The power of this method relies to a large extent on how well the matching is done.

Evaluation designs differ in their depth of analysis. *Synthetic* designs limit themselves to assessing the *general* effect of change programmes on job behaviour. In contrast, *analytic* designs identify and measure each of the main job changes and attempt to assess both their individual and interactive effects on each of the job behaviour measures. Common statistical techniques used in analytic designs are analysis of variance, causal path analysis and cross-lagged analysis.

The above four aspects of evaluation design combine to give four basic design forms: *synthetic before-after*, *synthetic control*, *analytic before-after* and *analytic control*. They vary of course in the degree to which they make demands on effort, skill and time, the synthetic before-after design demanding little, the analytic control design demanding much.[20]

The Hunsfos paper mill enlargement described in chapter 4 exemplifies the synthetic before-after design in action. The status of various performance measures were compared on a straightforward before-after basis; no attempt was made to measure the change variables.

Lawler, Hackman and Kaufman's (1973) evaluation of a redesign of telephone operators' jobs typifies the analytic before-after model.[21] They obtained detailed before-and-after measures of such intrinsic job characteristics as variety, autonomy, task identity, etc, and related these to before-and-after measures of motivation and satisfaction. Examples of the synthetic control model can be found in Paul and Robertson's account of the ICI job redesign programme. For example, evaluation of the effects of redesigning sales representatives' jobs took the following form: 'The experimental group ($N = 15$) was selected to be representative of the sales force as a whole in terms of age, experience and ability ... The rest of the sales force ($N = 23$) acted as the control group. The changes were introduced for the experimental group during December 1967, and the trial period ran from 1 January to 30 September 1968'. No specific measures of the job change variables were taken; the focus of interest was on general performance and satisfaction measures. Few published examples of the analytic control model exist in the field of job design, probably because of the difficulty entailed in applying the model in a practical work setting. Though deficient in some respects, Alderfer's (1967) comparison of enlarged with non-enlarged machine operator jobs, using detailed job content and satisfaction measures, illustrates the basic feature of the analytic control design.[22]

The main advantages and disadvantages of the four forms of evaluation design are summarized below:

	before-after	*control*
synthetic	Gives unreliable general picture, no certain cause-effect inferences possible; requires no special knowledge or methods	Gives reliable general picture of cause-effect relationships; requires only matched groups
analytic	Gives detailed picture, cause-effect inferences possible where appropriate statistics used; requires special knowledge and methods	Gives reliable, detailed picture, precise cause-effect inferences possible through use of matched groups and appropriate statistics; requires special knowledge and methods

Some organizational consequences

A required perspective in planned organizational change is to view the organization as a dynamic system with changes in one part of the system exerting effects on other parts. This applies especially to structural change such as is involved in job design. For example, the addition of discretion to jobs often means pulling down planning and control functions from higher-level jobs, thus flattening the organizational hierarchy. Beer and Huse (1972) report such a development at Corning Glass: '. . . at the beginning of the OD effort, the organization had a plant manager, a production superintendent, and three first-line supervisors, or a total of five supervisory personnel in the direct manufacturing line. As the assembly line workers took on more responsibility, the five have been reduced to three, the plant manager and two first-line supervisors).[23] It is for this reason that Myers argues that initial steps at job enlargement should be confined to improving existing jobs: 'This is least threatening or disrupting to job incumbents and their supervisors'.[24] Collapsing of higher-level functions can be undertaken later.

Another system effect of the Corning redesign was that 'as assembly workers took on additional responsibility they became more and more concerned about the total organization and product. 'Mini-gripes' turned into 'mega-gripes', indicating a change in the maturity of the assembly workers. At the same time, this freed up management personnel to be less concerned about daily assignments and more concerned about long-range planning'.[25]

Davis and Trist (1972) describe the system effect of a

job redesign in the Norwegian Industrial Democracy Project:

'The first experiment was carried out in the metal-working industry, a sector regarded as critical but requiring considerable rehabilitation. A rather dilapidated wire drawing plant in a large engineering concern was chosen on the grounds that if improvements could be brought about here they could be brought about any-where. Productivity increased so much that the experiment was suspended; the workers concerned had begun to take home pay packets in excess of the most skilled workers in the plant; a very large problem had now to be sorted out. Although the experiment confirmed earlier findings regarding what could be accomplished when alienation is reduced, it also revealed, for the first time, the magnitude of the constraints embedded in the wage structures and agreements which had been negotiated according to the norms of the prevailing work culture. The difficulty of changing such structure, which had enjoyed an enormous historical accumulation, accounted in considerable measure for the failure of earlier pilot experiments to spread'.[26]

Other system constraints have been noted in the enlargement of supervisory jobs in Shell U.K.:

'When a certain level of change implementation has been reached within a study area it begins to suffer from the contraints of other departments and areas outside it. This is particularly true of changes in authority to make decisions. Supervision in the study area find that they are making decisions which in other areas are made by the departmental manager. This means that in their dealings with other departments, they are having to relate at a higher organizational level. There are two inter-related consequences of this situation. The supervision being studied finds itself in an embarrassing position vis a vis its counterparts outside and frustration amongst the latter is aroused as a result. This problem can only be alleviated by extending areas of implementation as quickly as possible'.[27]

Job redesign invariably brings with it demands for a more participative and more interpersonally sensitive style of supervision. The supervisory role changes from the traditional one of controller of men, materials and information to one which serves to develop employee capacities through the coaching of new skills and the encouragement of independence in employees. In other words, the supervisor's responsibility becomes less concerned with specific parts of the work system and more concerned with its overall operation, particularly in mediating the relationship between the system's boundaries and its organizational environment.

Because the relationship between supervisor and employees under job enlargement becomes *consultative* instead of directive, interpersonal skills need to be cultivated. Emery and Thorsrud (1969) have also noted the need for interpersonal skills in joint consultation, emphasizing particularly the 'new relationship of mutual respect . . . presupposed by joint consultation'.[28] We may assume that this applies to an even greater extent in the specific context of the job relationship. In a study of a range of jobs in a manufacturing company, Alderfer (1967) found that holders of more complex jobs received less respect from superiors than did employees having smaller jobs. He suggested that the complex jobs have 'several sources of latent emotionality not found in the less complex jobs' but, because of organizational norms which forbid dealing openly with emotions, they were not exposed to rational examination. 'As a result, there were probably areas in most superior-to-subordinate relationships which neither party felt free to discuss. It would be quite natural for a subordinate to feel less respect from his superior because the superior did not fully share his views and information about issues which were important to the subordinate'.[29]

Job design and organization design

Organizational design, that part of organizational development which attempts to match organizational structures with relevant rask and environmental conditions, proposes that organizational effectiveness is a 'direct function of the structures it utilizes in applying its human resources to the task'.[30] Structures (the organizational relationships which coordinate people and their work) vary according to the type of task facing the organization.[31] Where task conditions are complex and dynamic, an *organic* form of organization is held to be most efficient; this is characterized by open-ended, flexible, participative structures. But where task conditions are stable and relatively simple, a bureaucratic form of organization is held to be most appropriate; here the structures tend to be rigid and hierarchical. Jobs in such bureaucratic systems should therefore be 'narrow, single-purpose categories of activities—coordinated at a higher level of hierarchy'[32]. This view of organization clearly jars with job design philosophy which assumes that, irrespective of differences in organizational task conditions, there is scope for redesign in most jobs. In fact, most redesigns have occurred in work systems where the task conditions have been relatively stable and straightforward precisely because their narrowly defined jobs were poorly motivating. The bureaucracy model need not contradict job design theory; its real significance for work system development lies in the nature of its 'limiting conditions'. The practical question for job design is: How far back can we push these limits?

REFERENCES

1 BENNIS W G, *Organization Development: Its Nature, Origins, and Prospects*, Addison-Wesley, Reading, Mass, 1969

2 WHYTE W F, *Money and Motivation: an Analysis of Incentives in Industry*, Harper & Bros, New York, 1955

3 DAVIS L E and TRIST E L, *Improving the Quality of Working Life*. Management and Behavioural Science Centre, University of Pennsylvania, Philadelphia, 1972

4 HERZBERG F, 'One More Time: How Do You Motivate Employees?' *Harvard Business Review*, Vol 46, 1968, 53–62

5 HERZBERG F, *op cit*

6 FORD R N, *Motivation Through the Work Itself*. American Management Association, New York, 1969

7 MYERS M S, *Every Employee a Manager*. McGraw-Hill, New York, 1970

8 HERZBERG F, *op cit*

9 WILKINSON A, *A Survey of Some Western European Experiments in Motivation*. The Institute of Work Study Practitioners, 1970

10 BEER M and HUSE E F, 'A Systems Approach to Organization Development', *Journal of Applied Behavioural Science*, Vol 8, 1972, 79–101

11 WALTON R E, 'How To Counter Alienation in the Plant', *Harvard Business Review*, Nov–Dec 1972, 70–81

12 KING D C, *Selecting Personnel for a Systems 4 Organization*. Krannert Graduate School of Industrial Administration, Purdue University, Lafayette, Indiana, 1971

13 WALTON R E and McKERSIE R B, *A Behavioural Theory of Labour Negotiations*. McGraw-Hill, New York, 1965

14 DANIEL W W and McINTOSH N, *The Right to Manage?*, Macdonald, 1972

15 PAUL W J and ROBERTSON K B, *Job Enrichment and Employee Motivation*, Gower Press, 1970

16 BEER M and HUSE E F, *op cit*

17 *Work in America*, Report of a Special Task Force to the Secretary of Health, Education, and Welfare, The MIT Press, Cambridge, Massachusets, 1973

18 Similar overoptimistic responses to social change programmes in general are discussed in some detail by SCHON D A, *Beyond the Stable State*, Temple Smith, London, 1971. See especially Chapter 7, 'What Can We Know About Social Change?'

19 CAMPBELL D T, 'Reforms as Experiments', *American Psychologist*, Vol 24, 1969, 409–429

20 GUILFORD J P, *Fundamental Statistics in Psychology and Education*, McGraw-Hill, New York, 1956

BLALOCK H M, *Causal Inferences in Non-experimental Research*, University of North Carolina Press, Chapel Hill, North Carolina, 1964

CAMPBELL D T and STANLEY J C, 'Experimental and Quasi-experimental Designs for Research on Teaching' in GAGE N L (ed), *Handbook of Research on Teaching*, Rand McNally, New York, 1963

LAWLER E E, 'A Correlational-Causal Analysis of the Relationship between Expectancy Attitudes and Job Performance', *Journal of Applied Psychology*, Vol 52, 1968, 462–468

21 LAWLER E E, HACKMAN J R and KAUFMAN S, 'Effects of Job Redesign: a Field Experiment'. *Journal of Applied Social Psychology*, Vol 3, 1973, 49–62

22 ALDERFER C P, 'An Organizational Syndrome', *Administrative Science Quarterly*, Vol 12, 1967, 440–460

23 BEER and HUSE, *op cit*

24 MYERS, *op cit*

25 BEER and HUSE, *op cit*

26 DAVIS and TRIST, *op cit*

27 *Releasing Supervisory Potential*, Shell UK Ltd, Stanlow, Cheshire, 1970

28 EMERY F E and THORSRUD E, *Form and Content in Industrial Democracy*, Tavistock Publications, 1969

29 ALDERFER, *op cit*

30 FRIEDLANDER F, 'The Relationship of Task and

Human Conditions to Effective Organizational Structure', Chapter 10 in BASS B M, COOPER R and HAAS J A (eds), *Managing for Accomplishment*, D C Heath, Lexington, Massachusetts, 1970

31 LAWRENCE P R and LORSCH J W, 'Developing Organizations': *Diagnosis and Action*, Addison-Wesley, Reading, Massachusetts, 1969

32 FRIEDLANDER, *op cit*

CHAPTER SIX

SOME RAMIFICATIONS

The economist Kenneth Boulding has described our age as the 'second great transition', by which he means the transition from civilized to post-civilized society.[1] This transition is dominated by technological developments unprecedented in scope and rate of change which are radically changing our social institutions. The technological and social effects of this trend have been examined in some detail by other writers under the term 'post-industrialism'.[2,3] The definitive features of post-industrialism can be summarized as follows:

1 Widespread use of technology has provided the means for the easy satisfaction of basic living needs, thus freeing man to pursue 'higher' interests
2 Emergence of new personal values characterized by desires for autonomy and self-actualization and suffused with an appreciation of people having interdependent fates
3 Environmental turbulence and technological excesses that make systems management more difficult and even threaten the future of our society

Post-industrial work designs

Such post-industrial conditions will demand new

organizational forms and values which run counter to prevailing organizational practices. Trist (1972) has contrasted the present and new organizational forms in the following terms:[3]

TABLE 4

Organizational philosophies and strategies in contemporary and 'post-industrial' societies

(*adapted from Trist*[3])

	Contemporary society	'Post-industrial' society
1	Mechanistic forms	Organic forms
2	Competitive relations	Collaborative relations
3	Separate objectives	Linked objectives
4	Own resources regarded as owned absolutely	Own resources regarded also as society's
5	Responsive to crisis	Anticipative of crisis
6	Specific measures	Comprehensive measures
7	Requiring consent	Requiring participation
8	Damping conflict	Confronting conflict
9	Short planning horizon	Long planning horizon
10	Detailed central control	Generalized central control

(*adapted from Trist*)

Work system design in post-industrial organizations will be based on 'open-systems planning' which has been described by Clark and Krone (1972) as a set of procedures whereby work groups can:

1 Rapidly identify and map out the dynamic realities which are in their environment
2 Map out how the organization represented by the members of the group presently acts toward and hence values those realities
3 Map out how the organization wants to engage with those realities in the future (ie, to set value-goals)
4 Make plans to restructure the 'architecture' of the organization in order to influence the environmental realities in the valued directions'[4]

FIGURE 3
(*from Clark and Krone,*[4] *reproduced by permission*)

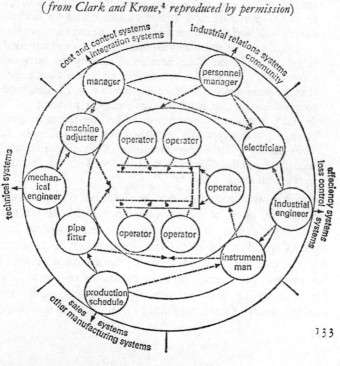

'Open' work systems require a high level of 'appreciation' of environmental conditions by their members so that all decision factors relevant to subscribed values can be evaluated and acted on.

In traditional 'closed' systems, members occupy narrow roles and appreciate only limited aspects of their work environment. Clark and Krone have depicted the essential elements of the 'closed' system in Figure 3.

> 'In the centre can be seen five "operators" who have been planned for by the five management personnel seen in the outside circle and maintained by the four maintenance personnel seen in the middle circle. The arrows going out from each person indicate the areas he is to appreciate and attend to, according to his job description and the other prescribed behaviours coming in from the different environmental domains attended to by the managers (illustrated in Figure by the outward arrows) . . . we would like to call attention to the fact that the organizational structure depicted . . . is designed to produce . . . constricted appreciation patterns . . . In fact, members attempting wider appreciation patterns . . . are typically punished for such offences as "rate-busing", "crossing craft-lines", "usurping management prerogatives", or just plain "sticking your nose in where it doesn't belong".'[5]

Clark and Krone go on to describe the practical features of open work systems 'in which the people who have direct responsibility for maintaining the flow of product of one form or another (a product concept can be the product of an information processing system, for example) also have direct responsibility for identifying and proactively engaging with the environments of that production flow'. In other words, system members appreciate and attend to many more spheres of organizational activity than they would in a closed system. The graphic of such a system is depicted thus:

FIGURE 4
(from Clark and Krone,[4] reproduced by permission)

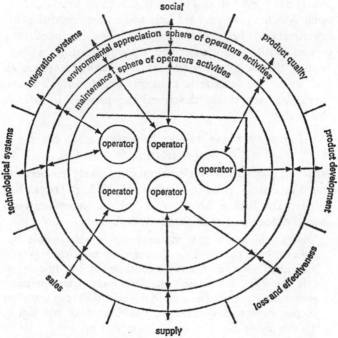

Krone has described an application of 'open systems' design to a Procter and Gamble production system in the United States where 'packing line workers identify, ahead of time, changes in sales volume, product formulation, social processes in the community, and so forth, and restructure their system so as to appropriately engage it with those forthcoming environmental changes.'[6]

The development of collective appreciative systems between individuals and groups requires sophisticated communication skills. Clark and Krone write of their own experience in this regard: 'We have learned and relearned what we should already have known, that open-systems planning is likely to be unsuccessful as an organizational intervention unless it is introduced into groups with well developed communication skills—groups, that is, whose members have learned to perceive and value one another's thoughts and feelings'. Clark (1970) has separately described the process by which this is done.[7]

Work experience and participatory democracy in 'post-industrialism'

Issues of participatory democracy are likely to become more salient in 'post-industrialism'. Vickers (1972) has focused the future problem as 'the antithesis between man the doer and man the done-by'.

> 'The age-long struggle to make power responsible has hitherto been the struggle to secure the political rights of individual men. For several centuries in the history of this struggle, it seemed that the only corresponding responsibility on the individual was the responsibility to be brave and watchful in the defence of his rights. This is evidently changing. Liberty is no longer to be bought at a price so relatively cheap and simple as "eternal vigilance". The aim of the ancient struggle needs to be restated. It is "to keep man the doer in the service of man the done-by, without frustrating either party in the process". This casts an increasing burden of responsibility on the "done-by", as well as on the doers'.[8]

Theories of participatory democracy argue that the done-by 'should receive some "training" in democracy outside the national political process' and that work organizations should be democratized to permit this socialization of participatory skills. Specifically, work experiences that help produce a 'sense of general personal effectiveness, which involves self-confidence in one's dealing with the world' generalize to a 'sense of political efficacy'.[9] Job design, therefore, will presumably assume an added significance in post-industrialism because of its ability to create a sense of individual competence which should help to extend the 'dialogue of the democratic process' and thus reduce the antithesis between doers and done-by. Walton (1972) describes two recent job redesigns which appeared to stimulate employee participation in civic and community affairs.[10]

Jobs in the advanced technology of 'post-industrialism'

There is a widespread, though ill-founded, belief that automation sweeps away routine manual jobs and leaves only jobs that are mentally challenging. This view is based on a perfunctory definition of automation, one which sees the process largely in terms of the mechanization of manual operations; it omits the automation of information-processing (ie, perceiving, deciding) aspects of work which will mark the next developmental stage of advanced technology.

The net effect of this process will be to divest direct operating jobs of their more important mental and manual attributes, as has been noted in the automation of a number of administrative and production functions.[11]

Planning of work systems to provide for human satisfactions will thus become a more refractory and pressing problem in the automated technologies of the 'post-industrial' future.

REFERENCES

1 BOULDING K, *The Meaning of the Twentieth Century*, Allen and Unwin Ltd, 1965

2 BELL D, 'Twelve Modes of Prediction', in GOULD J (ed), *Penguin Survey of the Social Sciences*, Penguin Books, 1965

3 TRIST E L, 'Aspects of the Transition to Post-industrialism', Part 2 of EMERY F E and TRIST E L, *Towards a Social Ecology*, Plenum Press, 1972

4 CLARK J V and KRONE C G, 'Towards an Overall View of Organizational Development in the Early Seventies', Chapter 11 in THOMAS J M and BENNIS W G (eds), *Management of Change and Conflict*, Penguin Books, 1972

5,6 CLARK and KRONE, *op cit*

7 CLARK J V, 'Task Group Therapy (I): Goals and the Client System', *Human Relations*, Vol 23, 1970, 263–277

CLARK J V, 'Task Group Therapy (II): Intervention and Problems of Practice', *Human Relations*, Vol 23, 1970, 383–403

8 VICKERS G, *Freedom in a Rocking Boat*, Penguin Books, 1972

9 PATEMAN C, *Participation and Democratic Theory*, Cambridge University Press, 1970

10 WALTON R E, 'How to Counter Alienation in the Plant', *Harvard Business Review*, Nov–Dec 1972, 70–81

11 COOPER R, 'Man, Task and Technology: Three Variables in Search of a Future', *Human Relations*, Vol 25, 1972, 131–157

International Labour Review, 'Effects of Mechanization and Automation in Offices: II', Vol 81, 1960, 255–369

Books from IPM

The IPM produces a large number of books on a wide range of management issues. Some of these are described below. For a free catalogue giving details of all our titles (over 95 now) write to the address on the title page. IPM books can be bought from your local bookseller or direct from IPM. Please add 10 per cent to cover postage and packing.

A Textbook of Personnel Management
George Thomason £3.95 (£5.50 hardback)

There have been books on manpower planning, books on training and on industrial relations, but there has long been a desperate need for a book which deals with the complex subject of personnel management as a whole in the British context.

Now at last there is a book to fill that gap – A Textbook of Personnel Management – written by Professor Thomason, Montague Burton Professor of Industrial Relations at University College, Cardiff. The author makes a thorough, detailed assessment of current personnel practice and describes how the function has become what it is. Professor Thomason's expertise in the legislative and industrial relations fields makes this book invaluable to the practising manager as well as to the student.

The Thomason textbook provides ideal background reading and will be indispensable for reference purposes. 536 pages. Second edition, revised throughout.

Recruitment and Selection
P R Plumbley £1.50

Philip Plumbley has revised this best seller, of which *Works Management* wrote: "This is one of the few technical publications which I have been able to read like a novel and I became so engrossed that I found it impossible to put it down until

I reached the final page. It was disappointing to find that it had come to an end."

Staff Appraisal
Randell, Packard, Shaw and Slater £1.30
Since this book was first published the authors have been involved in running some 60 courses covering over 500 managers, and the principles described here are now being used in several large organizations, notably the Delta Metal Company, Beecham Pharmaceuticals and Cheshire County Council. This edition has been brought up to date by incorporating the authors' latest thinking. "... useful to those planning a performance appraisal training programme ... written in a straightforward fashion and brings out some essential points of which any appraisal interviewers should have knowledge."
Personnel Psychology

"A very useful book which would be of tremendous help not only to those who may be responsible for designing and implementing an appraisal scheme but to every manager anxious to improve his skill in staff appraisal."
Industrial Society

A Practical Guide to the Employment Protection Act
Michael Rubenstein £2.00
On its way to becoming law, the Employment Protection Bill underwent many changes. Every manager will need to be fully aware of how the Act's provisions will affect his organization. Michael Rubenstein, a leading journalist in the field of industrial relations here provides expert commentary on the many different provisions of this complex and important new piece of legislation.

The Sex Discrimination Act — a guide for managers
Michael Nash £2.00
This IPM's guide to this vital piece of legislation will enable managers to assess the importance of the Act's provisions to their own organizations.

Developing Effective Managers
Tom Roberts £1.30

Although seven years have passed since the first edition of this book, the need for this kind of publication seems to be as pronounced as ever. The aim is to present, in as readable a form as possible, the main principles on which companies are basing their management development programmes and to discuss some of the more important problems and issues that arise.

This edition tries to incorporate new knowledge, new ideas and new thinking while retaining all that was useful in the principles and practices of seven years ago.

". . . packs into (its) most readable pages far more constructive ideas, lucid analysis and reasoned comment than many weightier volumes."
Technical Education

Personnel Management in Hospitals
Graham Millard £1.30

The book answers a lot of questions on a whole range of personnel management practices in hospital management such as recruitment and selection, training, staff appraisal, records, communications factors affecting morale and making the best use of staff resources. It also aims to promote discussion on practical aspects of personnel management and includes check lists and reference documents, plus some case studies to encourage the reader to relate to reality the range of sound employment practices explained in the book.

Practical Manpower Planning
John Bramham £1.50

This is an easily readable guide for the manager starting in manpower planning or wishing to know more about it.

Contents: 1 The development of manpower planning; 2 The manpower planning process; 3 Identifying manpower requirements; 4 Analyzing manpower supply I; 5 Analyzing manpower supply II – wastage analysis; 6 Formulating manpower planning; 7 Manpower control, reporting and costs; 8 Information for manpower planning;

9 Computers and models in manpower planning; 10 Future developments in manpower planning.

Techniques and Developments in Management — a selection
Margaret Butteriss £1.30

In recent years a bewildering number of developments in management practices have taken place, and every manager needs to be aware of the implications of these changes for his organization. Margaret Butteriss examines new practices which are intended to enable the individual to achieve greater satisfaction from his work, such as job rotation and flexible working hours, as well as techniques and developments which are aimed at achieving corporate needs. Every manager who wishes to keep abreast of current management issues will welcome this IPM paperback.

Basic Personnel Procedures
David Barber £1.00

From time to time personnel managers may find themselves in the position of establishing a personnel department from scratch, setting up basic personnel procedures or perhaps reviewing the organization of work in an existing department. This introductory booklet has been written with these particular problems in mind.

Instant Library?
A set of basic readings on a wide range of management subjects from *Staff Appraisal* to *Recruitment and Selection* in one easy move.

IPM's current catalogue now lists over 95 titles. A complete set of all our publications (everything listed in our new catalogue) is now available for the bargain price of £80 – normal cost over £150.

For details of IPM Courses and Conferences and our Appointments Service (90 per cent of all personnel management vacancies are carried in our journals), or for more details about the Institute itself, write to the address on the title page, or ring 01-387 2844.